Praise for Dr. Michael Fine and *On Medicine as Colonialism*:

"Michael Fine's *On Medicine as Colonialism* is a rich overview and critique of the US health care enterprise—certainly not a 'system' of care, but a fantastically costly conglomerate of multiple providers of health-related services that enriches them.... This is a sobering diatribe on health care in America, and it merits all of us fed up with the relatively low return on our investment in health to seek changes—to get more 'health' out of 'health care.'"
—David N. Sundwall, MD, professor emeritus of public health, University of Utah School of Medicine, and primary care physician

"Michael Fine has lifted up the hood of medicine's dysfunctional engine and explained how all the parts are working against us having a healthier population."
—Michael Rocha, MD, cardiologist

"*On Medicine as Colonialism* explains why our health care system has catastrophically failed.... It also explains how the flawed values of our medical care system infect the other systems in our society, compounding the problems. The Big Lie is that the 2020 presidential election was fraudulent. *On Medicine as Colonialism* reveals that the Biggest Lie is that our health care system is primarily concerned with protecting and improving health. The truth is, it's about money and power achieved by colonialist values and tactics. This book will make you angry—I hope angry enough to join others in advocating for change in the basic structure of our health care system."
—Edward P. Ehlinger, MD, MSPH, public health metaphysician

"*On Medicine as Colonialism* details the sociopolitical realities that undergird health injustice and offers a realistic perspective on achieving health equity."
—Jewel Mullen, MD, MPH

T0125035

On Medicine as Colonialism

Michael Fine

Foreword by Christopher Koller

ISBN: 978–1–62963–990–1 (paperback)
ISBN: 978–1–62963–994–9 (ebook)
Library of Congress Control Number: 2022943209

Cover design by John Yates / www.stealworks.com
Interior design by briandesign

10 9 8 7 6 5 4 3 2 1

PM Press
PO Box 23912
Oakland, CA 94623
www.pmpress.org

Printed in the USA

Contents

FOREWORD   Christopher Koller   vii

ACKNOWLEDGMENTS   xi

INTRODUCTION   Two Stories and a Definition   1

CHAPTER ONE   Medicine and Colonialism   8

CHAPTER TWO   Hospitals   17

CHAPTER THREE   Pharma and Pharmaceutical Retailers   36

CHAPTER FOUR   Specialists, Surgicenters, Radiologists, Cardiologists, and Tests   54

CHAPTER FIVE   Administrators, Consultants, Lawyers, and Doctors   67

CHAPTER SIX   Primary Care   75

CHAPTER SEVEN   Insurance Companies   82

CHAPTER EIGHT   Research   93

CHAPTER NINE   Medical Colonialism as, Well, Colonialism Itself   106

CHAPTER TEN   COVID-19   124

CHAPTER ELEVEN   Final Thoughts, Summary and
                       Conclusions, and a Little about How
                       to Fix This Mess   132

NOTES   137

BIBLIOGRAPHY   146

INDEX   148

ABOUT THE AUTHOR   153

Foreword

By mid-2022, at the time of this writing, coronavirus had claimed more than one million lives in the United States. On a per capita basis, that puts the country's death rate from the infection at three times Canada's, more than eight times Australia's, and ten times Japan's, Singapore's, and Taiwan's.[1]

And the toll is not even. According to the Centers for Disease Control and Prevention, American Indian, Latino, and Black populations are all about twice as likely to die from the disease as white populations.

This alone is a searing indictment of a health care system that consumes almost 20 percent of the country's resources.

How can this be? This is the question Michael Fine explores in this book. Fine approaches the question as Rhode Island's answer to Wendell Berry. Trading Kentucky's tobacco farms for the Ocean State's tenements, Fine brings Berry's deep respect for the value of human relationships and equally deep skepticism for the supposed benefits of our political economy to an examination of how health care is organized, financed, and delivered in the United States.

Fine is a physician by training and a novelist by heart, and his diagnosis is a metaphorical one—in the US, he maintains, health care has "colonized" whole communities. It is at first an odd analogy. In health care in the US, there is no invading force from a foreign land. There are no subjugated native populations. But the hallmark of colonialism, Fine maintains, is the use of power by outside entities for the purposes of wealth extraction from communities for personal or institutional benefit. And whether the community is defined geographically, ethnically, or economically, Fine asserts, the health care industry has succeeded magnificently at this process of wealth extraction.

In successive chapters, he analyzes how hospitals, the pharmaceutical industry, specialist physicians, the administrative bureaucracy, the hallowed (and hollowed) primary care sector, insurance companies, and biomedical research have allowed their public good functions to be perverted by an economic model that puts profits over people and turns care into a transaction. The result is wealth accumulation, uneven financial gains, and the impoverishment of entire communities.

The wealth that has been extracted by medical colonialism is not merely financial—although with over half of health care paid for by the government, it is indeed just our own money being moved around and accumulated. The real wealth is in the vitality of communities. In Fine's telling, towns and cities have replaced diverse small-business economies with ones based on medicine and education, where the only hope of economic mobility is a terminal job as a clinical assistant in a big health system. Repeatedly, health systems have extracted trust—an even more precious commodity—from Black and Brown communities, who have experienced persistent discriminatory treatment. The result is a collective loss of agency, of connectedness, and of hope.

Like his muse, Berry, Fine writes with the eye of both a humanist and a practitioner. He has worked these health care fields—as a clinician, public health official, and community organizer—and his passion for individual lives and concern for the common good is what drives his outrage at what has been wrought.

Health care practices its own version of manifest destiny. Its model of organization and financing is ineluctable in its power and direction, Fine maintains. This colonization may not involve invading foreign forces, but a group with power is seeking to impose its notion of what is good while enhancing its own personal wealth and status. And however well-intentioned its participants may be—the physicians, health professionals, scientists, and administrators who march forward as part of this force—they are doomed, like zealous missionaries, to create harm even as they labor to help. Colonization is inevitable, and "All our trusted health professionals and institutions are involved," he laments.

The abysmal performance of the United States in preparing for and responding to COVID-19 cannot be laid entirely at the feet of our health care system, however. Our cultural values and political leadership have both refused to realize our collective interdependence and the personal sacrifice that sometimes entails. As we shun limits on health care choices and budgets, so we shun limits on personal freedoms. Similarly, Fine's possible ways forward in his final chapter involve broad cultural reforms—and accompanying shifts in political and cultural power—far beyond the health care system. This continues his previous writing about the political engagement he thinks is required to construct stronger, healthier communities—ones in which wealth in all its forms is built, not extracted.

This prescription for a cure can be a tough pill to swallow for most people, who just want care and answers when they are ill and vulnerable and who often place their faith in the power of vague nostrums like "unleashing market forces" or "universal health care." It is no easier for the incrementally inclined health-reform advocates among us who promote technical changes like "bending the cost curve," value-based provider payments, patient consumerism, and evidence-based medicine. But a lesson from history is that few colonialists give up their advantages willingly.

Christopher Koller
President
The Milbank Fund

Acknowledgments

No book on healthcare in the US could be meaningful without the experience of the people and communities who interact with the health care mess we have—and survive anyway. I owe a tremendous amount to the people who've let me share their lives in small and large ways during my years of active practice—the people in Cleveland, Ohio; in White Mountain, Arizona; in Bethel, Alaska; in Portsmouth, New Hampshire; in Central Falls, Pawtucket, and then Scituate, Rhode Island; those in Sneedville and Rogersville, Tennessee; and in Dayville, Connecticut—and also in Glasgow, Scotland; Lugulu, Kenya; Buchanan, Liberia; Medyka, Poland; and Brava, Cape Verde, places not in the US but even more meaningful.

This book owes a tremendous amount to my teachers and colleagues in professional practice—those at Memorial Hospital Residency Program in Family Medicine; the Hancock County Health Department in Sneedville, Tennessee; Green Hollow Road Family Medicine; the Mansfield Health Center; Hillside Avenue and Community Medicine; the Rhode Island Adult Correctional Institute Medical Department; the Rhode Island Department of Health; Blackstone Valley Community Health Care, Inc.; and Jenks Park Pediatrics.

A George Soros/Medicine as a Profession Fellowship twenty-three years ago—led by David Rothman, PhD—and other fellows stimulated my early thinking about the meaning of medicine as a profession. Two months (over the span of ten years) as a visiting scholar at the Robert Graham Center let me explore many of these ideas. My colleagues and friends at the Association of State and Territorial Health Officers have challenged and inspired me over the years to think deeply and to see the world from many different perspectives, as have colleagues on the boards of the Scituate Health Alliance, Crossroads RI, RICARES, the Lown Institute, and the George Wiley Center.

I was exceptionally lucky to have spent time with Bernard Lown, MD, Jack Geiger, MD, and Jack Cunningham, MD, and even a little with Fitzhugh Mullan, MD, all of blessed memory. They each asked me to think deeply about the world we are made and the world that can be, and all left me and this world a better place.

The book wouldn't exist without the work and vision of Wendell Berry. His vision of community as "the commonwealth and common interests, commonly understood, of people living together in a place and wishing to continue to do so" and as "a locally understood interdependence of local people, local culture, local economy, and local nature" informed most of the thinking and critique in this book.[1] Robert Putnam's unroofing of the deconstruction on American communities was a wake-up call for me. And Bill Bishop's *The Big Sort* helped me understand exactly how those communities are being split apart.

Shannon Brownlee, Larry Bauer, Alan Ross, Beata Nelkin, Jewel Mullen, Ed Ehlinger, David Sundwall, and Chris Koller have been inspirations and coconspirators over many years. The ideas in this book are my fault. They have all tried to make them better, each in their own way, or showed me what true self-interested advocacy is really about.

Gabriel Fine pushed me to define colonialism more precisely. His intelligence and attention to the ideas in this book have helped me develop and understand them. No father anywhere has a better son (or daughter!). Scott Hewitt walks the walk of resisting medical colonialism every day, and I learn every day from his example.

Mayor James Diossa of Central Falls, Rhode Island, confronted COVID-19 with courage, and Mayor Maria Rivera and the Central Falls City Council brought amazing public leadership to the pandemic. They knocked on doors and staffed vaccination clinics—not a typical city government by any means. My colleagues at Beat COVID-19—(now State Representative) Joshua Giraldo, Elizabeth Moreira, Wilder Arbordela, Hugo Lopez, Tatiana Baena, Deborah Navarro, David Deloge, Scott Hewitt, and too many great volunteers to count—showed America what we can actually do when a community works together.

Paul Stekler and Gail Hochman have provided support and encouragement over many years. Andrea Chapin was a great editor. Gregory Nipper and Wade Ostrowski helped tremendously with line and copyediting.

Finally, Carol Levitt supported me in every way possible over forty-three years of working together and learning, and Gabriel and Rosie Fine have tolerated, critiqued, and encouraged this work, and inspired the rest of my life.

Two Stories and a Definition

In Central Falls, Rhode Island, where I work, the COVID-19 pandemic hit hard. People who live in Central Falls, the smallest and poorest city in Rhode Island, live in densely packed houses, often eight or ten people to a two-bedroom apartment, sharing one bathroom and kitchen. Many are undocumented immigrants. Most work two or three jobs to feed their families and send money home to family members in Central America, the Caribbean, or West Africa.

When Rhode Island shut down in March 2020, everyone forgot about the people in Central Falls. When Governor Gina Raimondo closed the state, she did everything she could to preserve the economy. That meant keeping essential services and factories open. Teachers, bureaucrats, administrators, lawyers, and even doctors started working from home. But the people of Central Falls kept working away from their homes—working with other people. Construction workers. Factory workers. Bus drivers. Certified nursing assistants. Store clerks. Landscapers. These people went to work every day, in part because they had to. Undocumented people don't qualify for unemployment insurance or stimulus checks. People in Central Falls kept working so they could pay the rent and the phone bill and buy food. Among people of color in Central Falls—who make up the majority of the city's population—only about 10 percent have the kinds of jobs that would allow them to work from home. Even so, 20 percent of the city's workers became unemployed, at least legally. Most people, employed or not, continued to work under the table if they could, just to make sure their families were fed.

So people went to work, and they got sick. By April 2020, Central Falls became the most infected place in the United States and one of the most infected places in the world. More infected than anywhere in New York City. More infected than Italy or Great Britain. More infected than Wuhan. We found out about how the virus was spreading the hard way, because there was almost no testing in Central Falls, at least at first. People died in their homes, afraid to seek medical advice. Whole families got sick. In those apartments of eight or ten people, many workers got sick at work, brought the virus home, and spread it to everyone in their households. In April 2020, there were four deaths at home from COVID-19, and doctors' offices were overwhelmed by the number of people who were ill and had no place to go.

In late April, after weeks of begging for help from the state health department, the state government, and the federal government, the cities of Central Falls and Pawtucket got together and stood up to create an Incident Command System (ICS), the usual response of emergency personnel to emergencies of various sorts, from fires and hostage taking to hurricanes. In those cities of one hundred thousand people combined, likely fifty thousand lacked primary care doctors. The local hospital had closed the year before after years of low occupancy, the result of changing demographics, poor management choices, and market-driven competition from larger hospitals just a few miles away. There was no one else to care for the population and no one else to fight the pandemic in the two cities. These cities had no public health experience and had never used ICS for a public health emergency, but there was no other choice: after weeks of begging, pleading, and cajoling state and federal officials, it had become clear that no help was on the way.

We'll do it ourselves, the cities said. *We'll use volunteers and city employees. We'll collaborate with community organizations, who we'll invite to the ICS from the outset. We'll build our own testing system. Our own phone consultation service, so that people who are sick can get medical help. Our own family support system, so that undocumented people can get food and cash to sustain them should they get sick. Even our own public health process to help people who are sick and in isolation and quarantine, because the state's isolation and quarantine systems have miserably failed. Our own data system, because there isn't much good data available about how the virus is infecting people in Central Falls and Pawtucket.*

The cities brought together those city workers and volunteers and built that system around a hotline inside of two weeks. I was the chief health strategist for the City of Central Falls as well as the health advisor to the mayor of the City of Pawtucket. I knew both cities well, and I also knew the health policy landscape at the state and federal level like the back of my hand. I had done my residency in the hospital that had closed, had practiced in both cities, and had served as the director of the Rhode Island Department of Health after that.

The ICS process worked like a charm. Inside of two weeks, we built a little health care system for one hundred thousand people that brought telephonic medical care, isolation counseling, testing, and family support to the people who got infected in the first wave of COVID-19. Four languages—English, Spanish, Portuguese, and Cape Verdean Creole—were available by phone. Our little health care system required only a phone number and a nickname from each caller—not even a real name, so we wouldn't scare off undocumented people. We had volunteer doctors, nurse-practitioners, and midwives on the phones. Volunteer premed students did isolation and quarantine counseling, helping people who were sick understand how to separate themselves from others so they didn't spread the disease.

The cities funded the process themselves in the short run—and requested $800,000 in state aid to make it sustainable. Over a billion dollars of federal pandemic aid flowed into the state in that period. Central Falls and Pawtucket hoped that a tiny portion of that $1 billion—less than one-tenth of 1 percent—would come to their cities so they could continue the critical public health work they had started pretty much on their own, when neither the state nor the federal government could organize itself to help protect the two cities' citizens.

But everything changed as soon as money came into the picture. There were meetings on top of meetings—not to respond to the public health emergency, but now to discuss the cities' request to fund their public health response. All of a sudden, as a budget was negotiated, there were lots of people on lots of Zoom calls. A new entity appeared in these virtual meetings: the local branch of a national organization called Local Initiatives Support Corporation (LISC), which is a housing organization, had contracted with the state to run something called the Pawtucket–Central Falls Health Equity Zone (HEZ). The state had decided to send all funds to LISC, not to either city. Everyone involved in the ICS process lived in or worked for the cities of Central Falls and Pawtucket, and most people (except me!) both lived *and* worked in one of the cities—and most involved were people of color who spoke either Spanish or Cape Verdean Creole. But none of LISC's employees lived in either city, and none of the LISC employees or any of the other state contractors—who worked for national consulting groups like the Boston Consulting Group or Alvarez & Marsal and who sometimes appeared as if from nowhere on these calls—either lived in one of the cities or spoke Spanish or Creole.

Finally, after *three months* of these calls, the state sent LISC $175,000 to use for the cities' pandemic response. Only $175,000, instead of the $800,000 the cities thought it would cost to run a full-fledged public health response. LISC made a deal with a large politically connected (and privately held) business headquartered in the one of the cities, a business that had been idled by the pandemic, to supply the 800 number and the information technology needed to run the hotline, and it also doled out money to community organizations that had been part of ISC and had been doing this work all along.

But when the $175,000 finally started to flow, it was too little and too late to stop the fall surge of COVID-19. And the money went not to the people of Central Falls and Pawtucket, but instead mostly to that large privately held corporation (a campaign contributor to one of the mayors), whose owners and most of whose employees lived in other places.

And then things got worse. While this process had been running with volunteers, a Latino guy who worked for the privately held corporation and lived in one of the cities had over-seen organizing and staffing the 800 number and the processes around that. As soon as the money started to flow, however, that corporation replaced him with a white guy who was the son of a friend of the owner and who lived in Rumford, a wealthy suburb a few miles away. While the process was running with volunteers, all the volunteers came from one of the cities. The moment the money started to flow, the privately held corporation wanted to use that money to bring back their own long-term employees, all of whom lived elsewhere, and it took a pitched battle to make sure that at least some of the people hired were from the cities, spoke the languages, and knew the culture of the places in which we were working. As soon as the money started to flow, the planning process went from almost all volunteer community people, deeply involved in the cities and community, to all white people who barely knew the cities at all—but who were all getting paid.[1]

In a few months, then, the little cities of Central Falls and Pawtucket saw a change from a mostly volunteer, locally initi-ated, locally run process of public health and self-defense to a poorly funded bureaucratic exercise that allowed state offi-cials to claim they were doing something and that resulted in cash flowing to people who lived outside the community and didn't really know the cities at all. People organized themselves to protect themselves and their neighbors. But as soon as the state became involved and money started flowing, the focus of the response flipped around. All of a sudden, the Incident Command System of Pawtucket and Central Falls, which had produced a little public health system called "Beat COVID-19" that addressed itself to a pandemic caused by a new disease that was infecting, hospitalizing, and killing too many people, many of whom were poor and working people, had become focused on contracts and cash flow, and most of the now-well-paid people who were involved were interested in the contract deliverables, not simply in what the community needed. Large sums of money were being moved about. But the process wasn't about the common good anymore. Or democracy. Or even about the incidence and prevalence of disease.

That was when a light went off in my brain. I had long understood that health care in the United States is a business, not a service provided for the public good, and that we have a medical services marketplace, not a health care system that cares for all Americans. But this experience let me see health care in a new way. What if health care was more than just a business? What if health care had become a false flag, a Trojan horse, a game of three-card monte? A way to use this pandemic to create income, a way to extract wealth from a community, or, worse, a way for politicians to attract attention to themselves so that they could advance their careers? The pandemic had attracted attention and money. When that money arrived, the smart set—people with one kind of power or another—figured out how to get that attention and money to flow their way. What if communities where the pandemic hit were just the raw materials of this process, the place where the gold is mined, the oil is extracted, the rubber or banana trees are grown, and the people are just the providers of labor and consumers of manufactured goods made elsewhere? What if medicine wasn't about health or health care or the pursuit of happiness or democracy at all? What if medicine was just colonialism? An excuse to extract the wealth of communities, one that destroys their ability to care for themselves in the process.

In a pandemic, and generally, we think of health care as a public good, a service communities need to be stronger and more resilient. But from research for my previous books, *The Nature of Health* and *Health Care Revolt*, I knew that health care in the United States has another function altogether. In the US, health care is a business that tends to make the rich richer and keep the poor impoverished. I learned this by following the money and by seeing who makes how much doing what—by seeing, for example, how hospital, pharmaceutical, and insurance executives and their shareholders make a ton of money while family doctors do okay but have to work all the time, while the nation struggles with income inequality, dropping life expectancy, and downright terrible health outcomes, especially among poor people and people of color.

But in the pandemic, I learned that the US faces a worse problem yet. In the pandemic (and for *fifty years* before that), people with power and money co-opted federal and state government and used state power to exploit the pandemic to make more money for themselves. The pandemic revealed what had been hidden from Americans in plain sight: that the health care profiteers have turned government into an agent of wealth extraction and have turned medicine itself into the excuse for government to do so. State power has turned health care profiteering, objectionable enough in itself, into colonialism—into a process that strips the resources from communities and leaves those communities with no agency and no ability to protect themselves, exactly what the old colonial powers did across the developing world.

In this book, I'll follow the money and show you what health care and medicine in the United States is all about.

CHAPTER ONE

Medicine and Colonialism

I had been working part-time at a community health center in Central Falls and Pawtucket, Rhode Island, for the four years just before the pandemic struck. Community health centers were invented in the mid-1960s (by Jack Geiger, MD, a mentor and hero) to help address the health impacts of racism by providing primary health care to the poor, to working people, and to anyone without a family doctor, many of whom are people of color. The community health center's staff was diverse. Most of the medical assistants, receptionists, and other frontline staff lived in Central Falls and Pawtucket. Some of the nurses did as well. But very few of the doctors, nurse-practitioners, or physician assistants lived in either city, and very few were people of color. None of the more highly paid administrators lived in the community, and none, not even one, were people of color. Too few members of the community health center's board were actual community members, and too few were people of color, even though by federal regulation, 51 percent of the board had to be "users" of the health center, a regulation the health center satisfied by the letter but not the spirit of the law. To its credit, and with a little pushing from me, the board had added four people of color from within the community, but it was still majority white, even though the main site of the health center itself is in Central Falls, which is 80 percent people of color.

This pattern—that the people who work in health care administration and leadership in hospitals and health centers live in other communities—pops up wherever medicine is practiced and wherever hospitals and doctors exist in the US (except, perhaps, in rural parts of the country, where there is no practical way for administrators and doctors to live in other communities).

Take hospitals. The executives of hospitals, their boards, and most of their doctors typically live in wealthy suburbs, while the poor and working people who make up the bulk of their patients live in poor and working communities near the hospital itself.

It's like that in community hospitals. But the pattern is much more apparent in academic teaching hospitals, which are often located in the midst of urban poverty: hospitals like Mount Sinai Hospital and Columbia University College of Physicians and Surgeons in New York, Johns Hopkins in Baltimore, Yale in New Haven, the Cleveland Clinic and University Hospitals in Cleveland, Boston Medical Center and Boston University Medical Campus, Rhode Island Hospital in Providence, and Hahnemann Hospital in Philadelphia (before it was bought and closed by a venture capitalist).

Though not all academic hospitals are in poor urban areas, the number of academic hospitals that are located amidst urban poverty is remarkable. Are those hospitals located in poor places just because poor communities have lots of sick people? Or is there something about academic hospitals that makes or keeps poor places poor? Most poor and sick people have Medicare and Medicaid, which pay for the care of the sick. If we think about Medicare and Medicaid as representing part of the wealth of those poor places—in 2022, they represent between $5,000 and $12,000 or more per person per year in most states—are hospitals stripping away some of that wealth, which could otherwise be spent locally, and carrying it to other places? Could it be that, yes, while those hospitals teach medical students and residents, they also use the cover of illness to extract funds from the federal and state governments and then send those funds elsewhere? Could it be that those hospitals are not just in the business of health care but are also in the

business of extracting wealth from the communities in which
they are located and moving that wealth elsewhere? Hospitals
extracting wealth from communities? Impossible! But if so,
that would make hospitals something other than health care
or medicine entities. That would make them like the gunboats
in the colonialist enterprises of yore, and it would make the
whole United States health care mess almost sound like . . .
colonialism.

What is medicine for, anyway? Most Americans think of medicine and health care as an essential public service, a common
good like education or fire protection. People know they cannot
survive injury and disease by themselves. Most of us know that
in order to survive and recover from illness, we need services,
expertise, medications, and attention. Health care maintains
life and helps people function in society. Life lets us have liberty,
and life and liberty together open the door to the pursuit of
happiness. So medicine helps us live and is part of what philos-
opher John Rawls called the "original position" of a democracy,
one of the essential services that gives us the ability or agency
to use our liberty to pursue happiness—and to sustain democracy itself.

    Most of us think, perhaps naively, that essential services
should be made available to every citizen without regard to
income or the ability to pay, just because they are required for
every citizen to participate in society and thus in democracy
itself. Police and fire protection are available without charge in
most American cities. The same has been true of elementary
and high school education for the past century. But medicine isn't provided equally to everyone without regard to the
ability to pay. The closest we have come to making medicine
equally available to everyone in the United States is a law called
EMTALA, the Emergency Medical Treatment and Labor Act of
1986, which made it illegal for hospitals to turn away people
with life-threatening conditions from their emergency departments. EMTALA, though, didn't make it illegal for hospitals to

charge those people as much as they wanted to, and emergency medical treatment is not the same thing as medical care, not by a long shot.

Even so, most Americans sense that some part of medicine is not about profit, likely because of the professional oaths that physicians take, which obligate them to provide medical advice without regard to their own ability to profit from that advice. So physicians, for example, are ethically obligated to tell you that doing nothing for back pain is usually the best treatment, even physicians who own an MRI machine that would generate profit for them if they recommended that MRI. And many physicians perceive that they have a professional obligation to unself-interested advocacy, which is a sense of obligation that goes above and beyond their actual oath and means that they see themselves as required to advocate for the needs of their patients, even when they have no self-interest in such advocacy at all. In addition, many people perceive that society should discourage people from profiting from the misfortunes of others, because it is just a hop, skip, and a jump from such profiteering to being willing to cause the misfortunes of others, a situation that would pull a society apart at its seams. (Other health professions have similar ethical obligations.)

On its surface, then, medicine seems to have nothing in common with colonialism, which appears to be completely about profiting from the misfortunes of others.

Colonialism—one nation-state conquering another place, replacing local government with the rule of an outside army or government, removing, under force of arms, the exportable value of the natural resources of the conquered country, and then profiting by selling back manufactured or other goods—is an activity of nations and places, not of individuals and their personal needs. The colonialist uses his (pronoun chosen consciously) military might and social organization to subjugate weaker places and to create profit and wealth for himself.

But the truth about health care, health professionals, and medicine, once you look under the hood, is that the health care enterprise is very far indeed from being not-for-profit and very far from serving the common good, at least in the United States.

In the US, we spend some 18 percent of the gross national product on health care, some $3 to $4 trillion a year, sucking up much of the excess value that the nation produces. Between 25 and 50 percent of all our health care spending on services and products is unnecessary or wasted.[1] That's $1 to $2 trillion every year—enough to send every high school graduate in the US to Harvard for free, or enough to house the homeless in the US three or four times over. Health insurers in the United States doubled their already billions of dollars in profit in 2020, in the middle of the pandemic, on top of spending hundreds of billions on administrative expenses (which includes the salaries of executives).[2] Pharmaceutical companies made $1.27 billion profit worldwide in 2020, before COVID-19 vaccines were available, and much of that came from the US.[3] "Nonprofit" hospitals' presidents make millions of dollars a year.

That means between $30 and $60 million is leaving each community of ten thousand people each year inappropriately, money that could and should be spent on schools, adult education, public parks and playgrounds, public housing, public transportation, libraries, and community centers, expenditures that make communities richer in the options people have and the opportunities to learn, grow, and spend time together. My little town of ten thousand spends about $30 million a year on everything it provides to the people who live here: on schools, on roads, on police and fire and ambulance service, and on garbage pickup. How much more we could do with another $30 to $60 million! Better schools, better recreation programs, adult education, better teacher and police salaries, and lower taxes to boot!

Suppose medicine does have this seamy underside. Suppose health care *does* extract wealth from communities. Does that make health care colonialism? Taking gold or iron ore out of the earth, as well as farming, which, at its core, uses labor, sunshine, and water to remove the wealth of the soil in the form of crops, are simplified examples of wealth extraction. Manufacturing is another form of wealth extraction. Manufacturers bring raw materials, buildings, light, heat, and machines together with people who need jobs and then use that combination to create a finished product that can be sold for more than it cost to produce, a process that extracts value from the labor of the people they hire. *Colonialism* is what happens when states use military power to extract value from other states or communities; *wealth extraction* is what happens when individuals use their resources, their natural advantages, and the law to extract the value of the natural resources of a place or to extract value from the labor of other people. Thus, colonialism is what happens when *states* use military power, and wealth extraction is what happens when *individuals* use other kinds of advantages or power. Colonialism and wealth extraction have different agents but similar results—both result in the wealth of communities and people being carted off by others for their own purposes.

It is worth considering here how colonialism itself has changed in the postmodern era. When nations had gunboats and were free agents limited only by what competing nations would permit without a fight, the nations with gunboats and armies conquered places where people were weaker and then carted off their wealth. In the process, the conquered nation lost the ability to make its own choices about the distribution of wealth—or anything else, for that matter. The conquered nation lost its *agency*. More recently, however, nations have been contained and often controlled by international trade agreements and by multinational corporations, many of which have budgets larger than some of the countries in which they operate.

So now the people who make use of state power have new and different tools to extract wealth from other countries and from communities inside their own countries. International trade agreements restrict access to markets by using the threat of tariffs that can be levied on the products of countries that don't join, making their products uncompetitive and unsalable abroad. Business conglomerates restrict access to transportation or processing facilities for raw materials and retail markets, using contract law to control supply and demand as they consolidate market power. Venture capitalists, private equity groups, and hedge fund managers lobby to change or subvert labor and environmental laws in their own interests, and they lobby international, federal, and state regulatory agencies to change regulations in ways that create a legal framework that supports those interests.

Colonialism can now be understood as a process that exploits state power in the service of profit. It removes the agency and resources of people in their own communities both domestically and abroad.

At the same time colonialism was changing, medicine morphed into health care and also changed technologically, economically, and politically. Medicine developed tools that were much more effective at preventing and curing disease, began to represent economically significant portions of nations' gross national product, and became a service provided or regulated by the state in most places.

The economic and political aspects of medicine and health care are most central to this discussion. Who goes to the doctor and pays cash on the barrelhead anymore? In some countries, the state provides health care and medicine to everyone. In other countries, payment for health care and medicine is provided by the state for some but regulated by the state for all.

As the face of colonialism around the world has changed from the use of military power to expropriate resources and enslave people in foreign places into the use of legal and economic power to expropriate resources and remove the agency of communities, the process of medicine has become a state function. Medicine, a service that saves lives, facilitates healing, and promotes recovery, changed from being provided for one person by another to a state-provided or state-supervised service made available to all or most people, with huge economic impacts because of its scale. And medicine and the health care enterprise that developed became something akin to a raw mate-rial, an exchange that has monetary value that can be mined or extracted, exploiting the people and communities in which governments and the world economy have invested with these health care dollars, which can then be carted off by some people interested in profit at the expense of other people who want only to live in their communities with one another, building wealth for one another as communities with agency.

That's the connection between medicine and colonialism. In the United States, Medicare and Medicaid, government programs, are the funders and regulators of much of the nation's health care spending (along with military and veterans' health care programs and state and local governments' purchase of health insurance). Even the purchase of health insurance by private companies is regulated by state and local law, and most people have some kind of health insurance, which means their health care choices carry monetary value that can either be invested locally or expropriated. Health insurance gives the health care profiteers a lever to use as they promote their prod-ucts and try to control the funds that flow around the purchase of those products, as insurance companies cover or are required to cover services as diverse as medications for Alzheimer's disease, vaccines against human papilloma virus, and infer-tility treatment.

As we shall see, health care profiteers use state power and the state's control of health care purchasing to extract resources from communities, resources that we see as dollars that pay for health services. In the process, those profiteers destroy the agency of local communities, which no longer have the resources they need to provide services to their own residents or make their own choices. To the extent that the health of communities is a function of their ability to make their own choices, exert their agency, and promote the way their residents take care of one another, medicine and health care have become antithetical to that kind of health, as medicine has become a tool of colonialism and is being used to deconstruct democracy itself.

In this book, I'll look at how medical colonialism works in the United States and explain how communities can stand up, take their health care back, and create a health care system that is for people, not for profit—and perhaps breathe new life into the cherished remnants of American democracy in the process.

CHAPTER TWO

Hospitals

O nce upon a time, medicine wasn't very effective at saving lives. A hundred years ago, we had no way to treat infectious diseases. Children often died from diphtheria and measles as well as from simple problems like infant diarrhea. Adults died from infectious diseases like pneumonia, influenza, tuberculosis, and rabies, as well as cholera, yellow fever, and even malaria (in the southern United States).

The infant mortality rate in 1900 was about 167 deaths per thousand live births by the age of one year; it is about 5 deaths per thousand live births today. Life expectancy in the US then was about forty years; it is now about eighty years for most people, although it's five years less for most Black Americans. Doctors could tell you how likely you were to die if you got sick, and they could give you cough syrups and other medications—mostly opiates—to make you feel better, but they couldn't often heal you.

Before effective general anesthesia and good antibiotics, surgery was a risky proposition. With the exception of simple surgeries like hernia repairs and the draining of boils and abscesses, surgery was saved for people who had no other hope. People with gangrene had legs amputated, which sometimes saved lives. But there was no heart surgery, no brain surgery, and very little cancer surgery, because surgery was often riskier than the diseases it was meant to cure.

Women in labor typically delivered babies at home, but many infants and mothers died in the birthing process. (About nine women out of a thousand giving birth in 1900 died, but 10 percent or more of women giving birth in the hospitals of the 1840s and 1850s died—many of whom had contracted childbed, or puerperal, fever, a common infection during hospital births in that period. Today we get very concerned when we lose one mother per ten thousand live births.[1])

Early hospitals were dangerous places. They were rife with infectious diseases, and you were as likely to die from being in the hospital as you were from the diseases that brought you to the hospital in the first place. Hospitals were places that housed the sick and dying poor, places that trained doctors, and places where doctors could see patients quickly and efficiently because so many sick people were gathered in one place. Much of what we know about the spread of infectious disease and antiseptic technique came about when Dr. Ignaz Semmelweis, in Vienna in 1847, realized doctors were killing hospitalized women in labor by infecting them with childbed fever, because the physicians hadn't yet learned to wash their hands between deliveries—and even then Semmelweis's colleagues thought he was crazy. He had a nervous breakdown from the pressure and died young, likely from an infected wound he got in an insane asylum after being beaten by guards.

There were two kinds of hospitals between 1751, when Ben Franklin and Thomas Bond established the nation's first hospital, in Philadelphia, and about 1950, when hospitals started to become corporate enterprises. Public and charity hospitals were places for poor and working people to isolate from their families when they got an infectious disease and to recover from accidents or injuries when they needed nursing care. Private "doctors' hospitals" were started by physicians looking to simplify their daily work and supplement their incomes. They were often just new wings built onto doctors' homes. Those physicians could see all their recovering (or dying) patients in one place, which made their workday more efficient. And they could make extra money charging for room and board. Over the years, some doctors' hospitals became nonprofits and raised charitable funds, but many stayed private and were sold to private for-profit hospital holding companies like the Hospital Corporation of America, which was founded in 1968, or Tenet Healthcare Corporation, built on a hospital holding company founded in 1969. Both came into being just after the creation of Medicare and Medicaid in 1965 and the entrée of the US government into medicine in a big way for the first time.

Public and charity hospitals were usually founded with public funds or were supported by charitable contributions from wealthy industrialists and other individuals, part of the noblesse oblige of the upper classes, who back then often felt concern for the well-being of the poor—or understood that much of their own wealth was produced by the labor of poor and working people who worked long hours in the mills. Those public and nonprofit hospitals gradually acquired significant assets— the land on which they sat and the buildings that composed them—and many accumulated significant cash assets because of donations made by philanthropists and grateful patients over the years. Indeed, five of the largest endowments of nonprofit organizations in the US are hospitals or hospital systems.[2] Many nonprofit US hospitals have endowments larger than $1 billion.[3]

So some hospitals were clearly community assets while others were owned by physicians and existed to serve physicians' interests. But in the years before 1965 or so, even the early doctors' hospitals were community based and community involved. They employed local people. They purchased most of the supplies they needed—linens and food—from local stores and local farmers. They put the money they earned into local banks, because big national banking corporations didn't exist yet.

In the years before 1965, both kinds of hospitals existed in communities and employed people from the communities they served. The interstates hadn't been built yet, so it was hard for doctors or nurses to live in a well-heeled suburb twenty or thirty miles away. There weren't very many hospital administrators making million-dollar salaries. There were only doctors, nurses, orderlies, and the like, not thousands of people employed to bill for hospital services or to do "corporate compliance" or to run complex electronic medical record systems, which exist in large part to fuel billing done by all those billers, who in turn are watched over by all those compliance people. There were no send-out lab tests, no distant medical supply companies, not many drugs, and no CT scans or MRIs.

Even so, in the years before 1965, hospitals evolved into the center of health care in many communities. Hospitals were places where doctors and nurses met and worked together. Many hospitals became concerned with the health of people in their communities, because diseases and conditions in those communities impacted the hospitals' workloads and need for resources. Hospitals developed emergency departments that became places for everyone in the community to use, open twenty-four hours a day, and that gave hospitals a sense of mission and a direct connection to the communities they served, whether those hospitals wanted that connection or not, a role written into statute by federal law in 1986.

But little of this evolution happened with much knowledge, forethought, or planning. As hospitals evolved, funding and regulation evolved with them. Hospitals appeared to be community resources, although the character of their connections to their communities varied tremendously from place to place. Few Americans, and fewer American policy makers, really understood what hospitals were, what they were capable of, how they functioned, and how they impacted the communities in which they were located. Most Americans don't know much about hospitals now, other than they are the place to go if you are in an accident or become seriously ill.

Americans don't know, for example, that most hospitals are completely private enterprises that operate with almost no public oversight of their funding, spending, or operations. Most of us also don't know that these private enterprises are publicly funded. Almost 61 percent of all hospital income is from public funds: from Medicare, Medicaid, the Veterans Administration, the Department of Defense, workers' compensation, the Indian Health Service, the National Institutes of Health (for the research that academic hospitals conduct), and from public employee health insurance at the local and state levels.[4]

Many people assume that most hospital income comes from private health insurance companies, but the overrepresentation of public funds in hospital revenue makes sense when you think about it. Old and poor people are the most likely to get sick enough to need hospitalization. Everyone over sixty-five has Medicare, and everyone too poor to afford health insurance on their own, or who works at a job that doesn't provide health insurance, qualifies for Medicaid. Medicaid insures about 50 percent of pregnant women. That means the US government pays for most hospital stays and so funds most hospital services.

But few people know that the US government exerts almost no control over hospital operations or choices. The government has no influence over what doctors or hospital administrators are paid, even though we fund their salaries.

About 80 percent of US hospitals are private, not-for-profit corporations, which means they don't pay taxes when they have income that is greater than their expenses. They are run by governing boards, usually made up of volunteers who are substantial (read: wealthy) local citizens who appoint themselves. That's right. Almost no hospital board members in the United States are elected by anyone other than existing board members, and most were recruited by the hospital CEO, even though most of the money they are spending is public money and even though they set the salary of the person who likely recruited them. These boards are charged by the tax code (and not any health care regulatory agency) with providing fiscal oversight and with making sure that hospitals achieve their stated missions. The boards decide on these missions themselves. Hospital missions usually involve providing quality health care to the people who live in a certain place and not turning people away because of their inability to pay, or some language close to that, although hospital boards are free to choose any mission they wish as long as that mission does not explicitly commit them to making a profit (if they are nonprofit organizations).

One community hospital I know, which started as a nonprofit serving a very poor and working-class community, was bought by a for-profit company and was then taken back to nonprofit status by its owner. He decided that the hospital's mission should change and now be to generate funds for poor people from the part of India he came from. And no one could do anything to stop him. (As I'll say again and again in this book, you just can't make this stuff up.)

There are state and federal regulations that require hospitals to function in certain ways: they can't discriminate against anyone on the basis of race, creed, color, or religion (now, that is, although until the 1964 Civil Rights Act, discrimination by race was actually baked into hospital funding by the Hill-Burton Act), they can't turn away someone in the middle of a life-threatening emergency, they have to adhere to certain standards of cleanliness and sanitation, they have to report medical errors, and so forth. After the Civil Rights Act of 1964 and its application to Medicare's passage in 1965, some hospitals became adept at institutionalizing racism by locating in or moving to places where there were few people of color or by the attitudes and actions of their medical and nursing staffs—and many other hospitals, founded by religious denominations to care for their coreligionists, made it clear by the icons on their walls and the attitudes of their personnel that people of other religions were not welcome.

But note that no state or federal statute or regulation requires hospitals to provide one kind of service or another, or to address themselves to the needs of one population or another, or to have any legal obligation whatsoever to provide a certain set of services to everyone living in one community. Instead, hospitals exist to sell services to whomever wants to buy those services and are free to charge whatever the traffic will bear.

In the US, then, we depend on the kindness of strangers to create and supply hospital services to the general population.

(Individuals with means are free to buy whatever hospital services they can afford.) There is no one responsible for making sure there are enough maternity beds. Or enough cardiac surgeons. Or enough brain surgeons. Or even enough primary care doctors. In the US, every hospital and every health care professional gets to do what they want, and only what they want, even though what they do is often (minimally) regulated once they choose to do it—*after* they choose to do it. There is no one to tell hospitals where to locate, how large or small to be, or who they must serve. No one is looking at the population of the United States and saying, "We need this many hospital beds here, and this many hospital beds there," or that we have more hospital beds somewhere else than we need. No one is in charge of saying we have enough primary care doctors or cardiologists or MRIs in one place but not enough someplace else.[5]

There is no one in charge of hospitals or, for that matter, any other health service in the US. Just someone in charge of writing the checks to pay for what we have, and others to moan about the absence of what we lack in the places that are underserved or have been abandoned.

Hospitals consume 30 to 40 percent of all health care spending in the US, money that too often leaves the communities in which that spending occurs.

Consider who works for hospitals and how they get paid. Most of the people in hospitals are certified nursing assistants (CNAs), phlebotomists, receptionists, maintenance people, and the orderlies who transport people and materials from place to place. Most of those people are local, and the bulk of that group is paid near minimum wage. The need for them—and they are all necessary, because they take care of people who are sick—is determined by the number of patients in the hospital, which is, to some degree, determined by the number of people who are sick at any given time. (Okay, maybe a third of patients in most hospitals at any given time don't *really* need to be there. Those patients are in the hospital because the hospital admits them to protect itself against malpractice, a practice that also happens to support its bottom line.) Still, because that large, low-paid group of hospital employees is very likely to come from within the community or nearby, their salaries may sometimes constitute waste but don't constitute expropriation. The money they are paid stays in the communities in which they work.

About 60 percent of hospital workers earn less than $50,000 a year. But about 10 percent make more than $100,000 a year, and of those, 2.8 percent made more than $200,000 in 2019.[6] Most of those making over $200,000 are hospital administrators and employed physicians. Nurses make up 28 percent of the hospital workforce and earned about $90,000 a year in 2019. When you do the math, that means that at least 22 percent of salaries are paid to that 12.8 percent of hospital workers—administrators and doctors, mostly, making more than $100,000 a year—and that underestimates the amounts, because many of the people making less than $50,000 a year make far less than that amount, and many of the people making more than $200,000 a year make far more, with senior administrators often making $1 million or more and many hospital CEOs making more than $2 million.

In 2017, the highest-paid nonprofit hospital CEO made $21.6 million, thirteen nonprofit hospitals paid their CEOs between $5 and $21.6 million, and sixty-one nonprofit hospitals paid their CEOs between $1 and $5 million. Of the eighty-two largest nonprofit hospitals studied, only six paid their CEOs less than $1 million. In this period, these hospitals' assets increased by $39.1 billion, a return on investment of more than 20 percent. These hospitals paid out $26.4 million for lobbying.[7] And that's only nonprofit hospitals, which must publicly report their CEOs' salaries and the salaries of their five highest earners. About 20 percent of hospitals are for-profit; their senior executives' salaries and profit do not have to be publicly reported at all.

In 2018, there were about 6.2 million hospital employees in the US, who in total earned about $364.2 billion.[8] Of that amount, 22 percent—or at least $80 billion, but probably more, and likely closer to $100 billion—was paid to hospital workers earning more than $100,000 a year. How much of that money stayed in local communities and recircled as local wealth? That is unknown, but it is hard to believe that much did.

No one knows how many highly paid employees live near the hospitals in which they work, but in most places, the more highly paid employees very likely live far from the hospitals in which they work, particularly when those hospitals are in densely populated poor communities. A fair amount of hospitals' money likely leaves the communities in which they are located, following hospital CEOs, administrators, doctors, and consultants back to the expensive suburbs in which most of those highly paid people reside.

This is not a zero-sum game, of course. There is nothing to guarantee that lower hospital costs would translate into lower copays and deductibles, lower out-of-pocket costs for consumers, and lower taxes and better public services, because the political process is complex, and politicians always fight over resources and rarely spend public funds in the most productive ways. But the constant demand that hospitals make for more resources certainly constrains the ability of employers, governments, and individuals to make different and better choices with their wealth.

How do hospitals expand the amount of money they extract from the public? How do hospitals maximize income? Hospitals, like every other marketplace participant, follow the money. They choose services that create the best return on investment (which they call "product" or "service" lines), not services that maximize the public's health. What services make the most money? Surgery. Cardiothoracic surgery. Invasive cardiology—cardiac catheterization and electrocardiology. Neurosurgery. Orthopedic surgery. Gastroenterology. Anything that involves a procedure. What services are so poorly paid they always lose money? Smoking cessation. Treatment for substance use disorder. Primary care, even though the number of primary care physicians per ten thousand population is the only health service that has ever been shown to measurably *improve* the public's health as it reduces cost. Why?

The answer to why some hospital services are more profitable than others is lost to history. It is due to a combination of factors: the risk of these procedures, which brings heightened emotional awareness about them and creates drama that in turn creates a perception of value; the long training time required for surgeons who practice these specialties, which allows them and the hospitals in which they practice to argue for better reimbursements; the role of Medicare in setting prices for procedures, prices that most insurance companies copy; and the role of lobbying by specialty societies and hospitals, which influences the choices made by Medicare in setting those prices.

At one level, hospital prices represent a kind of medical blackmail of individuals: if you are dying of something, or think you are dying, you will pay any price to stay alive. Hospitals are holding a metaphorical gun to the heads of people who are sick. Give us your money, they say, or we'll just let you die.

Grateful patients are often so relieved when they survive that they hand over their money and praise their doctors and hospitals to the heavens as they do so. (These patients often do not understand the extent to which their lives were really at risk. Sometimes, yes. More than occasionally, not so much.) In the background sits health insurance and the health insurance process, which removes the individual from having to pay those prices, most of the time. But the drama and the fear help drive a certain willingness to pay the prices hospitals ask, and that willingness drives insurance companies to pay those prices as well. Hospitals charge what the market will bear, and there are a host of others in the media and flitting around government who make sure that the market can and will bear a lot.

But at another level, hospital prices represent the intervention of the state into medicine and the health care process. Medicare sets prices. Hospitals and specialty-society lobbyists influence those prices. Medicare also structures the way hospitals bill for services, and all insurance companies and other health care bill payers follow Medicare's lead on this, using a standard billing form called an HCFA 1500 form (HCFA was the Health Care Finance Administration, an earlier name for the Centers for Medicare and Medicaid Services, or CMS) and mirroring Medicare's entire billing process, which uses diagnosis and procedure codes that the American Medical Association created but that CMS requires.

A host of administrators now exist to run the process of billing so that hospitals can increase their "take"; almost one-third of hospital staffs and salaries are now *billing people*—and most of those people and their huge costs exist because of the way government (via CMS) has structured the billing process. All those billing people are matched by administrators in Medicare, Medicaid, and insurance companies—people who decide how much of hospital bills should be paid and people to write the checks, people whose salaries we also pay, a veritable army of administrators, one that exists only to decide how much money hospitals will earn.[9] All of this financial activity is invisible to the public and appears inevitable to policy makers. Health care is complicated, Americans often say. Too complicated to change.

But to paraphrase Big Bill Haywood, when one person has a dollar they didn't work for, some other person worked for a dollar they didn't get. When hospitals generate huge cash flows, when society has to pay the salaries of administrators who plan profitable "service lines" (in hospitals!) and also has to pay for the administrators in Medicare and Medicaid to set prices and to adjudicate claims, when we support an army of administrators at insurance companies who duplicate the work of Medicare and Medicaid and develop and market insurance "products" as well, someone pays. Who pays? You and I pay. Communities pay.

Hospitals don't just profit by setting prices and through the billing process, though. Hospitals profit by driving the utilization of health care services, many of which are unnecessary and ungodly expensive. How do hospitals drive utilization?

Think of the billboards you see promoting hospital emergency departments on major (and minor!) highways. Think of the advertisements you see in newspapers, magazines, and online about specialized hospital services. "We have the best back surgery! The best neurosurgery!" they say. "Our emergency room will get you seen in thirty-five minutes! We have the best cancer care! The best cardiac care!" The subtext is clear: Come to *us* when you have a pain or a problem. Don't bother with your family doctor. Just use the emergency department! Have a headache? Come to our neurologists. Have back pain? Come to our orthopedists!

And that's exactly what people do now. They come to hospital emergency departments in droves. In 2018, there were 130 million visits to emergency departments of hospitals in the United States, but only 16.2 million hospital admissions resulting from those visits, or about 12.4 percent.[10] That means at least 114 million emergency room visits were likely not for emergencies!

But the whole truth about many of these conditions and diseases is never displayed in the advertisements. Ninety-five percent of back pain will improve by itself in thirty days. Most headaches are from muscle spasm and emotional stress, which aren't dangerous and so don't need a CT scan, an MRI, or a neurology consultation. Most chest pain isn't heart related (though chest pain in middle-aged and older people who have risk factors for heart disease can be life threatening and requires urgent intervention). Most people with angina don't need coronary bypass surgery *or* cardiac catheterization. By setting up emergency rooms and marketing those emergency rooms, hospitals have established a huge vacuum cleaner to suck in all sorts of people, both the sick and the "worried well"—a vacuum cleaner that gives hospitals the opportunity to use their CT scans, MRIs, specialists, and operating rooms to find and fix all sorts of problems, many of which don't need fixing but help them extract billions of extra dollars.

Yet hospitals are doing exactly what American culture has asked them to do, which is to compete and create profit. Most have little or no responsibility for or interest in the public's health or in making communities stronger or more vibrant.[11]

In January 2018, Hahnemann University Hospital in downtown Philadelphia was sold to American Academic Health System, a company controlled by Joel Freedman, the founder and CEO of Paladin Healthcare Capital. Hahnemann was just across the street from the Philadelphia Convention Center, right in the middle of downtown Philadelphia (aka Center City), and it was the closest hospital to swaths of the northern part of the city, where many communities of color lived. For years, Hahnemann had served the poor and working people of Philadelphia and trained thousands of young physicians.

Paladin was in the business of "turning around" old community hospitals, usually in communities of color. (It owned several hospitals in California, where Prime Healthcare, a company in the same business, also got its start.) Paladin had recently bought and successfully "turned around" Howard University Hospital in Washington, DC, the clinical home of Howard University College of Medicine, the most prestigious Black medical school in the nation and the hospital that serves much of the Black community in Washington, a city where health care is still shockingly segregated by history and culture.

The purchase of Hahnemann was funded by $120 million in loans from MidCap Financial, an affiliate of Apollo Global Management, one of the largest and most feared private equity firms in the nation, itself long controlled by a man named Leon Black, who stepped down from his role at Apollo after it was revealed he had paid Jeffrey Epstein $158 million for "tax advice." Black was the son of Eli Black, a Polish immigrant who once owned United Fruit, a company that was tied to the overthrow of the government of Guatemala by the United States CIA in 1954 and that became United Brands in 1970. Eli Black committed suicide in 1975 after learning that federal regulators were investigating allegations that United Brands was bribing Honduran officials. (Eli Black didn't buy United Fruit until 1960, however, so he can't be blamed for the US action in 1954. Even so, you just can't make this stuff up.) The loans MidCap Financial made to Paladin Healthcare Capital, Freedman's company, were at 9 to 10.5 percent interest, well above the market rate.

Freedman and Paladin failed to turn Hahnemann around. At the end of June 2019, Hahnemann declared bankruptcy and closed its doors. Freedman laid off the staff and auctioned off the residency slots, the Medicare-funded positions that paid the salaries of the residency physicians who do most of the patient care. Then he sold off the land and the buildings, which are being turned into condos.[12]

A great urban hospital closed. We'll likely never know for sure who won and who lost money on the deal. Certainly, a great deal of money changed hands. A hospital that had once been devoted to the care of the poor—a great community resource— is now being turned into condos where wealthy people are likely to live. What had once been ours became theirs. And it may well be that large profits were made by individuals in the process. Just maybe.

Venture capitalists, private equity firms, and hedge funds have recently figured out a number of ways to use hospitals to extract resources from poor communities. A number of entrepreneurs, many of them physicians, buy up distressed hospitals in poor communities and "turn them around" by running them like businesses, not like charitable organizations: Steward Health Care in Massachusetts, Prime Healthcare in California, Paladin Healthcare Capital, Tenet Healthcare in Texas, and many others. These firms are backed financially by some of the biggest private equity firms and hedge funds on Wall Street: Apollo Global Management, Harrison Street Real Estate Capital, Cerberus Capital (named after the many-headed dog that guarded the gate to the River Styx in mythological Hades, I swear!), the Blackstone Group, and many others.

These old hospitals get into financial trouble because technology has changed, and many services that were only available at hospitals—CT scans and MRIs, nonemergent surgery, laboratory studies, and colonoscopies—are now done safely and less expensively in surgicenters, imaging centers, and endoscopy suites. It is politically difficult to close old hospitals, because communities see hospitals as a critical resource (which they usually aren't) and a source of many jobs (which they are, even when the jobs don't contribute meaningfully to health outcomes and create unnecessary health care expense). Private equity principals and hedge fund executives understand that politicians will help support hospitals with tax money so that those politicians don't have to take on the politically unpopular but fiscally responsible task of closing hospitals that have outlived their usefulness. The politicians broker the sales of these hospitals to private equity firms, hedge funds, and their backers, changing laws and using tax treaties, tax-free municipal bonds, and deals cut with the retirement funds of hospital employees to get the regulatory approval necessary for a nonprofit hospital to be sold to a for-profit private owner. The private equity and hedge fund folks often agree to keep the hospitals open for a few years, which gives these politicians time to move on to other jobs before the new owner closes the hospital and sells the land and buildings.

Usually, in these transactions, no one notices that the hospitals were built with charitable assets, with money donated to a nonprofit in order to provide a public service: to create an institution that was supposed to serve the common good. These charitable assets are effectively public property and should be thought of that way. They are supervised by private boards, true, but the state has overall responsibility for assuring that those charitable assets are used in the public interest. The attorneys general of most states are responsible for supervising how these charitable assets are put to work in the public interest. Attorneys general are responsible, perhaps, but they are also elected officials, and most don't want a public hospital to close on their watch. No one wants to be the one to close a community's hospital, even if it is bankrupt. So no one looks at these transactions that closely, and no one really notices when the ownership of a once-public hospital changes hands.

The private equity and hedge fund folks know that the real estate covers their downside risk. If they are fortunate and make the hospital profitable, they will generate profit and have an asset they can flip. If the hospital as a business doesn't work out, they have the real estate, which they can usually sell at a substantial profit. Along the way, they usually take out huge loans, secured by the business and the real estate, and use those loans to pay themselves handsome profits. The hospital gets stuck with the debt, and far too often that debt ends up becoming a municipal or state responsibility, often because the state guaranteed the bonds to make the sale go forward or because the state oversight process confers liability for debt as defined by property law.

The new owners follow a predictable path. They cut out "unprofitable" services, like maternity care or specialty clinics that provide specialty services for the poor. They bring in billing consultants, who ratchet up what Medicare and Medicaid and private insurers are billed for services, often venturing into gray zones that turn out to represent fraudulent billing practices. (Prime Healthcare and Steward Health Care and many others have been sued or have settled with Medicare and Medicaid after their fraudulent billing practices were exposed.[13]) They market "profitable" service lines, such as emergency care, cardiac catheterization, and orthopedic surgery, which are vulnerable to overuse. They bargain with insurers for better payment, often recruiting nurses' unions and government officials to help as they threaten to close the hospital. And they speed up nurses and doctors: more patients per shift for nurses and more patients per hour for doctors.

Of course, the more the private equity and hedge fund folks profit, the more communities lose. When a mother with a crying baby goes to the emergency room at three o'clock in the morning rather than call her pediatrician or family doctor, that $1,000 or $5,000 unnecessary extra charge is paid by tax dollars and replaces a free service provided by that physician. When a fifty-year-old landscaper gets back surgery instead of physical therapy (which works better), that $50,000 charge is paid by taxpayers in the workers' comp process. In both instances, the profit for the private equity and hedge fund folks goes up, as those folks accomplished what society asked them to accomplish: they made the hospital profitable. But the cost to society increases markedly, and resources that we should be devoting to public schools or public transportation or building community centers ends up in the pockets of the private equity and hedge fund folks instead of creating wealth for the community. What's worse is that all this wealth transfer is the transfer of public funds, transfers that occur under government supervision and are often facilitated and encouraged by the state itself.

There is more profiteering and wealth extraction in hospitals than any of us can imagine. Management contracts divert funds and make profitable hospitals appear unprofitable. Sweetheart equipment and staffing deals are covers for laundering money extracted from hospitals and the communities they serve. Through a complex set of contracts and loans, for example, Steward Health Care was started in Massachusetts by cardiologist Ralph de la Torre with money from Cerberus Capital. Steward is now based in Dallas. It bought up a number of old community and Catholic hospitals and took them private. Steward received funding from Medical Properties Trust (a real estate investment trust with a market capitalization of over $13 billion that owns hospitals in the United States, Europe, and South America and whose CEO earns about $17 million a year) to continue operations when it got into financial trouble.[14] It sold much of its real estate to the trust and now leases the real estate back. Medical Properties Trust owns 10 percent of Steward, which is privately held. The cash from the sale of the real estate became available to Steward's owners (including Medical Properties Trust) to do with as they pleased—to pay down debt, for example, or to take out as profit or as contracted income. All a bit of a shell game, on the surface, and one that seems irrelevant to the public discussion about health, health care, and profit, until you realize that this "real estate" was once public property and is now in private hands and that public money funds all these shenanigans—that it is all money from Medicare and Medicaid, with a little insurance-company money thrown in. That money represents the pooled resources of working people, supervised by a public regulatory process.[15]

And then, when a hospital that was once public or nonprofit but is now for-profit finally starts to go bankrupt, every politician for miles around, attorneys general included, runs for cover. There is the inevitable announcement: that the hospital will be merged and its services transferred elsewhere, or just closed. The local politicians are relieved that the private equity and hedge fund folks and not the local politicians themselves get blamed for the hospital closure. The private equity and hedge fund folks feel very sad and deeply guilty about being the ones to pull the trigger and announce the closure. Guilty, all the way to the bank.

We could have it another way, of course. There is nothing in the Constitution of the United States that says hospitals must be private nonprofit corporations with self-appointed boards that spend public money and have virtually no public oversight (other than the oversight to prevent them from actively harming or abusing patients).

Imagine we had a health care system for the United States instead of just a market for medical services. Imagine that all hospitals in the United States were not only funded by tax dollars (as they already are[16]) but were funded directly, without the armies of administrators who exist only to bill and pay hospitals and to increase their incomes. Imagine that hospitals were owned by taxpayers and governed by publicly appointed or elected governing boards accountable to the public for their fiscal oversight and focus on mission. Imagine that the mission of hospitals was to improve the public's health, not improve their cash flow and profitability, and to insure the wise use of community resources. What size would hospitals be then? How might they work in close collaboration with primary care doctors and the public health sector? And then imagine hospitals that build community collaborations, serve the public's health, and work to create community resiliency and a richer community life instead of just profiting from the misfortunes of others.

It isn't difficult to imagine a health care system that is for people, not for profit. Unfortunately, in a world of stakeholders and huge cash flows, it is almost impossible to imagine how we might get from where we are now to where we can and should be.

It *is* very difficult to see how we might change from being a nation that cannibalizes its communities and its citizens under the umbrella of medicine and health care to become a nation in which people in communities take care of one another and build wealth, measured as rich interactions between citizens and their environment, so that we all get better and stronger together.

But perhaps imagining is the first step to seeing, and seeing is believing, if acting and acting up are part of the process of belief.

CHAPTER THREE

Pharma and Pharmaceutical Retailers

The poster child for and the most glaring example of wealth extraction and the problem with pharma is the story of prescription drug addiction and overdose death. More than 10 percent of the general population is susceptible to drug and alcohol addiction, whereas 90 percent of us are not susceptible.[1] That means that 90 percent of us can have a drink, take a pill, smoke a joint, or even snort cocaine, and we get a little high and that's it. One and done. But for 10 percent of us, as little as one pill, one drink, one toke, or one snort opens Pandora's box, a door that is extraordinarily difficult to close again. For the susceptible person, that one use launches a biochemical and psychological cascade that rapidly turns into an irresistible urge and then often into a trip through hell. Most of us can partake without consequences. But some of us are vulnerable to addiction from the least exposure, the way people who are highly allergic can die from anaphylactic shock after the least exposure to any substance to which they are allergic.

For most of the last hundred years, the period in which addictive chemical substances have been easily refined and widely available, there has been a black market in drugs and alcohol, a black market that has sapped the wealth of communities by draining money and productive energy away from the more than 2 to 3 percent of us who are addicted at any one time.[2] In response, too many communities created an ill-considered approach to fighting this cancer, our so-called war on drugs—five generations of toxic policing and a gulag of prisons

that cost an unbelievable amount of money and that incarcer-
ated five generations of Black and Brown men and women. The
drug trade and our industrialization of arrest and incarceration
was bad enough already without help from legal, organized,
for-profit business.

But then pharma got involved.

In about 1996, a few pharmaceutical companies, led
by Purdue Frederick but also Johnson & Johnson, Teva,
Mallinckrodt, and others, apparently got jealous of the drug
dealers' profits and moved into the opiate business themselves.
They used clever marketing and positioning to change the rules
about legal opiate prescribing so they could sell more of these
addicting drugs legally.[3] In 1996, Purdue Frederick and other
pharmaceutical companies entered into relationships with the
Joint Commission, the accreditation agency for hospitals, which
is a partnership between the American Medical Association,
the American Hospital Association, the American College of
Surgeons, the American College of Physicians, and the Canadian
Medical Association. Pain suddenly became the "fifth vital sign."
The whole medical world saw its mission change from saving
lives to treating pain, a clever sleight of hand that encouraged
more opiates to be prescribed. The pharmaceutical companies
argued that opiates weren't addictive when used to treat pain,
basing their claims on two flawed studies from the 1980s, but
they backed up these claims with drug-company dinners and
slick advertisements in medical journals.

Before long, doctors were handing out opiates for sprained
ankles and mild back pain, both very common problems, and
soon, millions more people were addicted, first to prescribed
opiates and then, when the supply of prescribed opiates was
cut off by public health authorities, to heroin and fentanyl, a
synthetic opiate (when fentanyl became available on the street
in about 2012). By increasing the prescribing of opiates, these
pharmaceutical companies exposed millions of susceptible
Americans to addiction. By 2006, the number of people dying
from prescription drug overdose began to increase. By 2011,

drug overdose deaths in the United States had doubled from
ten years earlier.

But the point of discussing prescription drug addiction and
overdose death here is not to beat up on the pharmaceutical
companies, which have been sued, bankrupted, and indicted for
their behavior—although many of their owners and stockholders
still walked away with huge profits, unindicted and unscathed,
not like millions of families and communities across the US. The
point of discussing prescription drug addiction and overdose
death is to reflect on who paid what and who profited how in this
process. When someone becomes addicted to prescription drugs,
they become a regular user, and a regular user is a consumer.
You don't sell them one pill or one bottle of pills. You sell them
several bottles of pills a week and hundreds of bottles of pills a
year. For example, among people in Rhode Island who got opiate
prescriptions from five or more prescribers in 2015 (a good but
imprecise way to identify people who are addicted), the yearly
expenditure per person for those opiates was $927.76, versus
$64.17 for the average purchaser of any opiate prescription. In
Rhode Island, the cost of prescribed opiates in one year, in 2015,
was more than $44 million.[4] Total US spending for opioid anal-
gesic prescriptions increased substantially from $2.3 billion in
1999 to $7.4 billion in 2012. In 2016, Medicare Part D paid almost
$4.1 billion for 79.4 million opioid prescriptions for 14.4 million
Medicare beneficiaries, or about $280 for each person who was
prescribed any opiate—and that was only people with Medicare,
or about 18 percent of the population.[5] In fiscal year 2013, there
were 636,000 people enrolled in Medicaid with opioid addiction,
and $9.4 billion was spent on their care, although only about
9.7 percent of that was spent on prescription drugs and not all
on opiates.[6] There's the rub. The more people who got addicted,
the more opiates pharma companies sold—and the more other
drugs they sold as well, as people with addictions also develop
a host of other chronic diseases (or have them to start with).

In this way, addiction is a paradigm of colonialism itself.
You invade a country or addict a people to a substance. You use

force or the inherent force of addiction to make sure people buy what you have to sell. Money that was theirs becomes yours. You cart off all the resources of a country, or all the resources addicted people have. And you create a huge mess: polluted streams and polluted air where mines or oil wells used to be, or a black market, a corrupted culture, the destroyed bodies that addicted people are left with, and families and communities that have been ravaged in the process. And then you leave. You live somewhere else, where the water runs clear, where the air is pure, and where you don't have to deal with the burden of a ravaged earth or sickened people and wrecked families.

Of course, not all pharmaceuticals are opiates, and not all people and communities who use medications are addicted. But that business model—get people to depend on costly medications they will use daily—is exactly the business model pharma has chosen for itself. The most profitable pharmaceutical companies are not companies that develop and sell antibiotics that treat infections for a week or ten days or companies that develop vaccines that a person might use once in a lifetime (although, for manufacturers of vaccines during a pandemic, when the potential market is the population of the world, vaccines are a profitable business indeed). The most profitable pharmaceutical companies are those that develop medications for diseases and conditions that people will have their whole lives, like diabetes, high blood pressure, heart disease, multiple sclerosis, or schizophrenia. That we have evolved a culture to produce products that cause or contribute to the development of some of these diseases and conditions—namely high blood pressure, diabetes, and heart disease—is a different problem, one I've described elsewhere, and not the fault of the pharmaceutical companies. But pharma certainly profits from the diseases caused by the products our culture sells.

It is more than a little painful to note that many of the same people who own the stock of the corporate food enterprises, the cigarette companies, and the media companies whose products cause or contribute to the development of diabetes, high blood pressure, and heart disease also own stock in pharmaceutical companies. We've created a cycle of economic cannibalism in which some people create the misfortune of others and then profit from that misfortune, a society in which some suck the blood of the rest. Shame on those who engage in that, and shame on us all for permitting it.

Such a situation is not likely to be sustainable, but for the pendulum to swing the other way, it will take either a true social movement and profound political change or social instability and lots of violence. In the interim, we will have done serious damage to the natural world, causing climate change and pandemics, the first of the new ten plagues of the modern era.

Pharmaceutical companies are also adept at driving up prices, calculating what the market can bear. Some medications used to treat diabetes, which was once treated with insulin for pennies a day, now cost $500 to $1,000 a month. The medications used to treat hepatitis C cost $80,000 for a full treatment when they were released. EpiPens, used by children and others with allergies, used to cost $20 or $30 each but now cost hundreds of dollars a pop. Inhalers, used by people with asthma, used to cost $20 or $30 but now go for over $200. And so on. These stories have been told over and over in the popular press, but the telling hasn't slowed the explosion of cost one bit. And it hasn't slowed the wealth extraction that is the flip side of that cost either.

But what has not been well told in the popular press is the way drug companies manipulate the market to raise prices—and their profits. When a generic manufacturer creates an inexpensive version of an expensive medication that is about to go off license, the name-brand manufacturer buys out the generic manufacturer and takes the inexpensive drug off the market so that people have to buy the more expensive version. Drug companies frequently enter into contracts with pharmacy chains, pharmacy benefit managers, and insurance companies, deals that put only one drug company's brand of drugs in a chain pharmacy and that raise the cost to the patient because no other options are available. Then the drug company pays the insurance company, pharmacy benefit manager, or retail pharmacy chain for doing so, either in the form of discounting their contract price or directly in cash for entering into such a contract, and that payment stays with the insurance company, pharmacy benefit manager, or retail pharmacy chain as profit (because the payment isn't attached to the cost of each prescription), effectively fleecing the patient, who ends up paying the extra cost.

What do pharmaceuticals cost us? The United States spent $329 billion on medications in 2018. For individuals, pharma's cost is quantifiable. Between 9 and 16 percent of the health care dollar goes to pharmaceuticals.[7] If we were all a little below average, let's say about 10 percent of the $12,000 per person cost of health care in the United States, or about $1,200 per person per year, goes to medications. Or around $5,000 per family per year for a family of four, though most families experience much lower costs because most medications are used by older people. Still, $1,200—or $5,000—is a significant amount of money. Not enough to buy a new car each year, but almost enough to lease one, at least for a few months. Not enough for a house, but enough for a decent vacation.

But pharmaceuticals, you might argue, help people to function. They prolong the lives of people with chronic diseases like diabetes, high blood pressure, and heart disease and help people with other diseases like rheumatoid arthritis, multiple sclerosis, and sarcoid to function, to work, and to vote. They prolong the lives of people with cancer. True enough.

And don't medications help people live longer and more prosperous lives? Actually, yes and no. But likely more no than yes. There is no evidence that drugs extend the life expectancies of populations or make nations and communities more prosperous. Vaccines help to stop pandemics, and vaccines likely contributed to the expansion of life expectancy between 1900 and 2000. Drugs have theoretical individual and population health benefits as well as some risks—addiction, side effects, and cost diversion, which is what happens when we spend money on medications with little or no benefit but then don't spend money on public services that extend lives, improve the function of individuals and the community, and create a more equal and more sustainable community. Life expectancy is falling, not rising, as drug prices go up. We've made spectacular gains in extending the lives of some people with life-threatening diseases or conditions. But at the same time, we've experienced spectacular losses in our ability to be one people with shared resources, problems that show up as substance abuse disorder and opiate overdose deaths, as suicide and mental and behavioral health disorders, as obesity and worsening heart disease and stroke, and as being so spectacularly divided that we couldn't defend ourselves against a pandemic caused by a cold virus. So one step forward and two or three steps back, from the perspective of pharmaceuticals, drug prices, community, and public health outcomes over the last thirty years.

Put another way, individual drugs may help certain *individuals* to live longer and more productive lives, but the net effect of the *pharmaceutical industry* we've created, funded, and enabled is *measurable harm* to the public's health—and apparent harm to democracy itself.

Note as well that almost none of the money spent on pharmaceuticals stays in the community in which the person who buys them lives. If you build a house, most of the sale's price goes to excavators, carpenters, roofers, plumbers, electricians, painters, and even real estate brokers, most of whom are likely to be local, and so the money you spend recirculates in your community. (That money used to get deposited in the local bank—though very few banks are truly local anymore, which is another set of problems—so it could then be lent out to other people in your community who wanted to build homes of their own.) It gets spent at the local cleaners, in local restaurants, at local mechanics, at the local beverage store, at the local bakery, in the local hardware store, at local cinemas, and at the local lumberyard, although way too much is now spent at big chains of one sort or another (see banks, above—too few locally owned *anything* anymore), such as Home Depot or Lowe's, movie theater chains, chain donut shops, and chain restaurants, too many of which are fast food and make high-calorie junk. If you eat in a local restaurant, there's a good chance that the owners and staff are all local and the money recirculates, and even some chance that they buy food from local farmers, if there are any still left in your community. The same is true with the local hardware store, bakery, and lumberyard.

In a certain way, drugs are like cars, chain restaurants, and industrially produced food-like products that you buy in the grocery store. When you buy a medication, the landlord of the pharmacy may be local. The pharmacists and clerks in the chain drugstore are likely to be local as well. But the owners of the drugstore—very probably CVS, Walgreens, or Rite Aid—are very unlikely to be local, and there is only an infinitesimally small chance that the people who developed, manufactured, and marketed the drug are local. The cost of producing drugs is usually tiny—the bulk of what you spend is for marketing, packaging, distribution, research and development, deal cutting, and an exceptionally large profit margin. And most of that—manufacturing, marketing, packaging, R and D, and deal cutting—happens elsewhere. So the bulk of that $1,200 per person per year leaves your community, and your purchase makes someone far away richer but doesn't make your own community stronger or more resilient. That's wealth extraction on a good day, but it's colonialism when Medicare and Medicaid are the payers, when the state uses its power to collect taxes and FICA (the Federal Insurance Contributions Act, which takes an extra 1.45 percent of your paycheck and 1.45 percent from your insurer, or 3 percent off the top of your weekly or biweekly paycheck) from you and me and pays out that tax money via Medicare and Medicaid to drug companies, using retail pharmacies as the conduit and almost always insurance companies to process the paperwork. All legal. Nice work if you can get it. And quite a racket, once you understand the working parts.

But pharma spending is not just about the cost to each of us. Note that a *community* of one thousand people spends $1.2 to $1.8 million a year on drugs and medications. A community of ten thousand people spends $12 to $18 million. The unanswerable question is whether that money could or would be spent in another way and benefit that community more.

So pharmaceuticals have no clear public health benefit for communities. But the cost of drugs drains communities of their resources.

The net effect of pharma on communities is negative. Cost equals wealth extraction from poor and less resilient communities because of the way we've allowed the health care market to run up the cost without requiring a public health benefit in return.

It's not just drug manufacturers either. Drug manufacturers are just part of a massive pharmaceutical-industrial wealth extraction complex. The profiteers include retail pharmacy chains, pharmacy benefits managers, and a host of other middlemen agents and brokers who exist completely under the public's radar but whose profits flow to all these entities every time a person takes medicine or gets a shot.

Everyone knows the pharmacy chains CVS, Walgreens, and Rite Aid, which long ago displaced local drugstores run by local businesspeople in most communities. (Walmart also runs a robust pharmacy business in most of their stores, and there are also chain pharmacies now often located in many supermarkets.) All the pharmacy chains are in the business of selling medications, toiletries, food, and other products, using medications as their anchor—as the products that bring people into their twenty-five thousand stores all across America—so they can sell everything from vegetable seeds to toothpaste to feminine hygiene products, and driving the prices for those other goods up as well, as people will often pay more for nonpharmaceuticals at

PHARMA AND PHARMACEUTICAL RETAILERS

retail pharmacies because of the convenience that such one-stop shopping affords.[8] Again, when people pay more for goods and services, they—and their communities—keep less, and they sacrifice wealth and resiliency in the process. CVS claims that 82 percent of all Americans are within five miles of a CVS, a claim they used to justify becoming a major supplier of COVID-19 testing to the population of the nation, perhaps exploiting their market power and their relationship with US Secretary of Commerce Gina Raimondo—a former governor of Rhode Island, where CVS is headquartered—to make their point.[9]

When I was the director of the Rhode Island Department of Health, from 2011 to 2015, I had oversight of the state Board of Pharmacy and the health facilities licensing process when CVS applied to open MinuteClinics in Rhode Island, where the chain has huge political sway. After three weeks of intense study, I approved their application but tried to impose some conditions they didn't like, because I wanted to make sure we studied the impact of MinuteClinics on the rest of the health care delivery system, on costs and outcomes, in response to concerns expressed by the Rhode Island Academy of Pediatrics and others. (Their CEO called the governor three times a day after I rendered my decision—and got through every time. You just try *that* as a citizen and voter.) CVS threatened to pull 250 jobs out of the state if the conditions stayed in place. I got to choose between my job and conditions that, though wise, weren't certain to have much impact. I chose the job because of other important work we were doing, picking my battles for once in my life. (Evidence over time showed that retail-based clinics do drive up cost without improving population health, as I suspected they would. We still don't know their impact on continuity of care and on prevention.[10])

During the same period, the Board of Pharmacy used state law and state regulation to tightly restrict who could dispense medication in every setting, to make sure that only pharmacists could dispense, even though physicians, PAs, and nurse-practitioners could give out samples and inject vaccines and were trained to counsel patients about the risks and benefits of all medications. The board ruled against a community health center that cared for the poor and had been dispensing medications for tuberculosis and sexually transmitted disease so that patients could get started on those medications right away, a good way to ensure that they took at least some of these important medications that not only help cure disease but also help prevent its spread, protecting the public's health. From the perspective of the Board of Pharmacy, the law said only a licensed pharmacist could dispense medications, and that was important to the board. Yes, that rule prevented some dispensing mistakes. (Pharmacists, though, make plenty of dispensing mistakes themselves, even though they are trained and licensed. They're human!) But that rule also protected pharmacists' jobs and their monopoly over prescribing. In this case, the board's position was injuring the public's health. I did everything I could to change, and then work around, that ruling, but I never succeeded—the pharmacists and the chain pharmacies used their political power to stop me. Even worse, they used that power to prevent community health centers from dispensing needed medications to poor people, proving once again that some health care organizations and some health professionals have no shame when power and money are on the table. State power was used to protect income and profit, one more tiny way that medicines themselves are used to perpetuate medicine as colonialism in fact.

Market power turns into money. Money turns into lobbying. Lobbying is effective at trumping the public interest. The state becomes an instrument to create and perpetuate profit, one that aids and abets the extraction of wealth from communities or even one that extracts wealth from communities itself. So profit is protected, common good is jettisoned, and democracy goes out the window, all at the same time.

How do pharmacies impact communities? On the benefit side, pharmacies help people with chronic diseases to participate in community life, as discussed above. Pharmacies are businesses that pay taxes, and for most people, having a drugstore in the community is a good thing, because that way people don't have to drive long distances to get their medications. People meet in the drugstore, so pharmacies themselves are places that promote interaction and relationships. Pharmacies employ people. Not a lot, but some.

But on the cost side, pharmacies market and sell more drugs, which drives up the cost of health care. The retail-based clinics drive cost up more, and they likely disrupt the public health process a good bit by disrupting the relationship between individuals and their family doctors, a relationship we need to get prevention done and done well.

Most people don't even know that pharmacy benefit managers (PBMs) exist, but they are huge businesses, adding cost for patients and lifting resources out of communities. PBMs are businesses that contract with insurers (and other entities called third-party administrators, organizations that pay claims with other people's money, both employers' and insurers') to create formularies that define which drugs will be paid for, how much the pharmacy gets to keep, how much goes to the drug company, and what the patients' copays and deductibles will be. PBMs also negotiate many of the rebates (which some characterize as kickbacks) described above and below. If you think this is incredibly complicated, you're right! And if you think all this complication costs Medicare, Medicaid, patients, and communities plenty, well, you're right about that too. The process of drug utilization management adds an estimated $93 billion per year to US health care costs.[11] That's an amount larger than the state budgets of all but the four largest states.[12]

Pharmacy benefit managers have become some of the biggest corporations in the US. Two of them, CVS and Express Scripts, are listed among the top fifty of the Fortune 500 largest corporations in the world, although CVS also runs drugstores, which accounts for much of its size. And three out of the top ten Fortune 500 companies, and eight of the top fifty, are health insurers, PBMs, or drug distributors.[13] The money that funds these big corporations and all the profit they generate has to come from somewhere, and that somewhere is from you and me—and from the communities in which we live.

All the economic activity PBMs generate is added cost, different ways of making money out of inconsistencies and inefficiencies in the pharmaceutical market. But though that activity may save some money for someone at some time, the sum total of that activity is to add cost to an already-costly process. Remember, when one person has a dollar they didn't work for, some other person worked for a dollar they didn't get. And when one community gives up its resources to provide profit for big corporations, that community becomes and stays poorer in resources, in resiliency, and in relationships—and everyone in that community loses the richness of a life lived with other people in a way that is sustainable over time.

Could we have it another way? Can we imagine a world in which drugs contribute to the wealth of individuals and communities instead of being used to extract their wealth?

Having it another way is hard to imagine. Drugs are not vegetables or fruits. Many economists think that communities would benefit if we grew more food locally, that we'd have better nutrition if people ate more locally grown fruits and vegetables and a stronger local recession-proof economy if more people worked growing that food. But none of that is true for pharmaceuticals. There is no practical way I can think of to make research and development of new drugs local or to make their manufacture and distribution local. Drugs will always be developed and manufactured in a few central locations.

This makes them a cost center, from the perspective of communities, and fixed overhead for our society and our nation. That means that we as a nation need to work out ways to develop needed new drugs and distribute them, because they are needed to help some people function. How should we develop new drugs and produce the medications people need—and control those costs in the process?

First, we need centralized purchasing, so that we buy drugs for the nation and not person by person. For-profit drug companies hate this idea. The only way the Affordable Care Act of 2010 got passed was for President Obama to buy off Big Pharma, trading group purchasing by Medicare and Medicaid for the support of the pharmaceutical companies. Otherwise, Big Pharma would have used all its considerable lobbying muscle to block passage of the law. But turn that on its head for a moment. Big Pharma wasn't afraid of bulk purchasing for no reason. Big Pharma fears bulk purchasing because it knows the practice will reduce its profits. But reduced profits for Big Pharma means significant savings elsewhere—for the nation, for families, and for communities.

We were already in a bad place if one industry can use its financial power to block the will of the people and a process that would have benefited everyone. But that's who we are and where we were. Now we need to bring back group purchasing for all medications and make that the law of the land.

Second, we need to outlaw rebates, kickbacks from Big Pharma to PBMs and from Big Pharma and PBMs to retail pharmacy chains, as I described above. We also need to outlaw the kind of market manipulation by drug manufacturers we've seen when they buy up generic drug makers and put them out of business or when they acquire the rights to a so-called orphan drug and then increase its price 1,500 percent, using FDA regulations to prevent community pharmacies from compounding these medications from commonly available and inexpensive materials. (I told the story of one such manipulation, the story of KV Pharmaceuticals and Makena, aka 17-hydroxyprogesterone, in *Health Care Revolt*.[14])

We have an FDA and a Federal Trade Commission. Let's change the laws so these important regulatory agencies can do their jobs and prevent the manipulation of the market—and keep the playing field fair and level—to give all Americans a fair shake. There should be no room for anticompetitive behavior on the part of pharma, big or small. There is no excuse for kickbacks or side deals in medicine or health care in the United States. Let us bring our commitment to real competition and a level playing field to the table, develop a little backbone, and make drug companies play by the same kind of rules that high school baseball players play by: no knuckleballs, no spitballs, and no spiking the catcher.

Then, if there isn't adequate generic-drug-manufacturing capacity in the private sector, we need to build a public corporation to do that for us, analogous to the public option being considered now in many states for health insurance purchase, the one that was under consideration in 2010 and was then blocked by the lobbying of the health insurance companies. Most drugs are cheaper than water to make, and much cheaper yet to make in bulk. If some medications are a public good, then the public needs to organize itself to provide those drugs at low prices to all Americans. Once upon a time, we made unprofitable vaccines at public-university medical schools and pharmaceutical schools. Let's wake that process up and manufacture generic drugs at our universities. It's a great training process for pharmaceutical students and would likely provide jobs for thousands of kids who want to work their way through college so that they don't graduate with overwhelming debt.

And we ought to just give away generics, most of which are cheap to make. When you go to the doctor, you should walk out with your prescription for free, most of the time. The rules about drug dispensing were made by pharmacists for pharmacists, first, and then expanded by retail pharmacy chains to create a monopoly for themselves on drug dispensing, most of which is pretty simple and very routine if you use prepackaged generics. Sure, for drugs that might be dangerous if used incorrectly, let's keep dispensing them by pharmacists in a pharmacy. But Tylenol? (Tylenol is actually quite dangerous if used incorrectly but has been available over the counter everywhere anyway—another lobbying success by a rich old pharma company.) Oral contraceptives? Amoxicillin? Hydrochlorothiazide? Atenolol (the most widely used blood pressure medication)? We've been held captive by a for-profit industry that has monopolized common sense, and it's time we took back reasonable control of our own lives.

We need to be thoughtful about patent protection for new medications. Remember that there is no evidence that drugs and medications other than vaccines have extended average human life expectancy by one day, and yet there is plenty of reason for thinking that our current process is one of the many forces behind the shortening of that life expectancy and the compromise of public health that has accompanied the growing income and wealth inequality in the United States over the past thirty years. A little patent protection for new drugs, completely developed by private enterprise, seems reasonable. But we should not offer patent protection for me-too drugs like Lopressor, Toprol XL, atenolol, and Inderal, which are all beta blockers used mainly to reduce blood pressure and control heart rate, or Prevacid, Prilosec, Protonix, AcipHex, and Nexium, which are all proton-pump inhibitors used to reduce stomach acid and which also all do pretty much the same thing.

And we should not offer patent protection for drugs that do the same thing as existing medications but that only offer a little more convenience or some modification so that you only have to take them once a day or even once a week, modifications that have no new or different clinical or population health impact. (That's any drug with an XL, XL PR, or XR after its trade name, which means extended or prolonged release.) Our legal system, which represents state power, has been manipulated by drug companies to give them the ability to use patent protection, FDA approval for orphan drugs, and the manipulation of the tax code in the pursuit of more profit. That's colonialism. We need to stop that kind of manipulation and stop it now.

We contribute markedly to the development of new drugs by funding foundational research at NIH and at universities and medical schools. Reviewers at the CDC, FDA, and elsewhere in government contribute to drug development by establishing criteria for effectiveness and by spending thousands of hours reviewing and critiquing submitted documentation. True, drug manufacturers pay for that time in the fees they pay for drug approval. But we the people support the overhead of the government that has created the infrastructure to make drug approval possible. Those reviewers often help by suggesting changes in study design. Why shouldn't we get a little return on *our* investment? Most of the scientists who participate in the research were trained at public expense, via federal grants and scholarships or periods of time working at NIH or at other federal agencies. Patent ownership should reflect that material contribution. When public dollars contribute to the intellectual property created by the discovery of a new drug, a portion of the ownership of the patent should accrue to the federal government, even if that portion is small.

Finally, the drug development research enterprise should be community based and employ residents of all our communities. There are many for-profit research "shops"—usually run by physicians or other licensed clinicians—that recruit research subjects for clinical trials. The process of recruiting and paying subjects is now poorly regulated and supervised by proprietary institutional review boards (IRBs)—and the subjects recruited rarely reflect the diversity of our nation's population. All institutional review boards should be publicly appointed and community based and should employ people from all our communities, not just university-affiliated communities. IRBs should be independent and funded by fees from drug companies looking to run trials. They should have the power and the responsibility to require diversity of the patient population, to require translation so that speakers of many languages can be included, and to ensure fair payment to subjects so that people who are poor or substance dependent are not exploited in the research process. IRBs should also require true informed consent so that research subjects are not pushed into trials by clinician researchers whose careers and incomes hinge on the recruitment effort, trials from which the subjects will receive no likely clinical benefit.

But even more important, we need to work harder at prevention and community development, community by community, so that fewer people ever need expensive drugs. Better access to locally grown fresh fruits and vegetables. Community centers where people can learn and play together, where there are sports teams and options for exercise, one in every community, for adults and kids. Primary care centers in every community, so everyone is immunized and so we help everyone make healthy choices, guided by their own elders, friends, and neighbors, who we can employ for this purpose. More public transportation to help people walk a little more and to help people spend more time together. Better schools run by local people for their own kids, using standards they think are important. The list goes on and on. Big Pharma is the symptom, not the disease. We've let our common life slip away and then allowed ourselves to be drugged into forgetting what we've lost—and then we've let ourselves be medicated out of our despair, sadness, and grief. But drugging ourselves isn't working either. What we've lost is gone. The despair is real. The anxiety throughout our culture is endless and palpable.

There *is* a better way. It isn't medications produced by people who manipulate markets in the fearless pursuit of profit. It isn't substances to get people high so we forget about what we've lost. It isn't new toys to keep adults entertained so they work to get more of the same. It's a community of people, acting meaningfully together, making their communities rich, resilient places by the work they do together to make them so.

Not capitalism. Not socialism. Just a decent life lived by decent people who aim to come together in communities of people taking care of one another and to keep getting better and stronger every day.

CHAPTER FOUR

Specialists, Surgicenters, Radiologists, Cardiologists, and Tests

The Ochsner Medical Center in New Orleans is one of the many thinly veiled profit-making health care enterprises that leverages medical science to make money, often by doing acceptable-to-good-quality medicine for the rich. Ochsner. Mayo. The Cleveland Clinic. MD Anderson. Memorial Sloan Kettering. Kings and princes are drawn to these places. Dictators and foreign generals. Russian autocrats. Those of us who think seriously about health care and public health can see them coming a mile away. Swishy rooms. Concierge attention. Cash on the barrelhead. They usually have well-deserved reputations for being "excellent," which means having creature comforts for patients and medical or surgical staff with impressive credentials, reputations they create themselves by sophisticated marketing and by careful attention to discouraging poor people from coming anywhere near them, all of which helps create the country-club atmosphere.

Ochsner is in the second rank of these places, good but not the best, mostly a legend in its own mind. Founded by five surgeons in 1942, all from the Tulane faculty, the Ochsner clinic created, how shall we say it, an alternative for people who did not care to spend close-up and personal time with the tired, the hungry, the poor, the huddled masses who used Charity Hospital, then one of the great public hospitals in the United States. Ochsner is now ranked number 1 in Louisiana by *US News & World Report*. Not-for-profit now, which to most health policy experts means Ochsner doesn't pay taxes. Its profits are very likely drained off as salaries to administrators and doctors, a nice little game of three-card monte that hides profit behind salaries so the tax man doesn't have to see what seems plain to the rest of us. Ochsner has one person of color among the twenty-nine members of its executive leadership—the "diversity" officer—and one Asian person in that group. It does have some women, though. In 2017, two members of its seventeen-member board were Black. FYI, in 2017, New Orleans was 59.5 percent Black—for those of us who don't know segregation, institutional racism, and wealth extraction when we see it.

I'm sure Ochsner's very well-paid PR people would take issue with most of this description. And truth be told, I've never set foot in Ochsner, although I walked by it recently in New Orleans while doing research for another book.

The Ochsner pattern is one I saw hundreds of times while I was practicing primary care and public health. Once upon a time in Rhode Island, most orthopedists didn't take Medicaid, and poor people with broken bones or another orthopedic issue had to go to the resident-run clinics at the hospital for any orthopedic problem. The wait was months—four to six months or more for broken bones that heal in six to eight weeks—and there were no other options for people without insurance and those on Medicaid. In these clinics, which existed mostly to train new orthopedists, you didn't get assigned your own doctor. You saw whichever resident was assigned to that clinic on the day of your appointment. If you called the clinic, they didn't call you back, even if you were a family doctor calling about a patient. And in the unusual event a family doctor got through to talk to a resident physician, the resident of the day didn't know one patient from the next. If you were a patient calling about a problem, you had to wait until the resident on call got out of clinic or the operating room before they called you back, if ever. You could try to make an appointment in an orthopedist's private office, of course, but usually they had ways of making sure no poor people came to those offices. They'd want to verify your insurance up front, for example, and if you had

Medicaid, they'd send you to a public clinic. And there were lots of insurance plans they didn't accept. Or they'd tell you that a new-patient visit was $300, and you had to pay that up front before they'd make an appointment. Or they'd require a referral from your family doctor, and they'd keep a list of the family doctors whose patients they'd take referrals from. They knew which doctors had "good" practices and which ones they "didn't work with": those who worked in poor neighborhoods or for community health centers. Many problems healed on their own while people were waiting—if they didn't get worse and require the emergency department. Sometimes patients died while they were waiting to hear back about an appointment or for a return call about a problem, although people usually don't die from orthopedic problems, thank God. Not usually.

It turns out there is no rule that requires specialists—or any health professional—to see any patient who asks to be seen or is referred. It is perfectly legal for specialists and other health professionals to cherry-pick their patients based on what patients can pay them and on how that payment will be made—cash, credit card, insurance, Venmo, or Bitcoin. Specialists and other health professionals can do or not do whatever they want, as long as they do no harm. (Which insurance they accept turns out to be a pretty big deal for specialists, because insurance companies vary all over the map in terms of what they pay, how they pay, and their myriad rules about payment and patient care, so doctors have learned to be choosy after generations of abuse by these companies.) The relationship between specialists and insurance companies is generally not regulated by either state or local government. If you think health care referral and payment feels like the Wild West, with everyone doing exactly what they want when they want to do it, that's because it is completely disorganized. We have a market, not a system, and we have let the market organize our health care. Or not.

It isn't just many orthopedists who pick and choose their patients, though for many years orthopedists did this kind of thing more than most specialists. Now almost no psychiatrists take Medicaid or Medicare or insurance—you have to pay with cash or with credit cards. And there are lots of specialty hospitals like Ochsner and zillions of outpatient surgical centers that do the "wallet biopsy" up front. Want cataract surgery? Insurance or pay up front. Want in vitro fertilization? Cash or insurance up front. The way Ochsner or the Cleveland Clinic or any of a hundred private specialty hospitals operate is no accident, from a business perspective. You maximize profit by making sure that your customers can pay high prices. To the extent that society has made sure that some kinds of people from certain communities have money, you work to include them. If that means turning away whole communities of people who don't or are unlikely to have money, so be it. You can't make money caring for people without the resources to pay for their care. Without margin, there is no mission. That's the language that lots of people in health care use. But if the purpose of health care in the United States is to create profit, which it is, then the margin *becomes* the mission and there is no reason to care for anyone without resources.

As states turned to private insurers for the administration of Medicaid, what is known as Medicaid managed care, places like Ochsner found ways of caring for people with that insurance, despite a history of making sure "those people" went elsewhere. That doesn't preclude them from having concierge floors—or even suites—where the wealthy can pay for the creature comforts of fine hotels. In cash. For services not covered by the kind of insurance most of us have. The more things change, the more they stay the same. That said, there *has* been progress providing specialty care to working and low-income people and people of color. But there are still stark differences in access to and utilization of many specialty services, just as there are stark differences in the United States, where our health outcomes vary tremendously by race and income, so that white people still live on average five years longer than Black people and so that the infant mortality rate among white babies is one-third the infant mortality rate among Black babies. In the US, there are still huge disparities in the medical services offered to people, with white and wealthy people getting quick and easy access to expensive services like kidney transplants and heart surgery while poor and working people of color are offered more profitable but usually time-consuming and uncomfortable options like kidney dialysis or medications to control crippling angina.[1]

If you think medicine is a business, then it makes perfect sense to pick and choose your clientele. Most people think any specialist or health professional should be able to decide how many patients they want to see and where or when to practice. If you think medicine is a business, then it makes perfect sense to practice in a rich suburb, where geography makes it more convenient for patients with resources to see you and the usual absence of public transportation makes it difficult for poor and working people and people of color to get to your office. The practice of medicine in the US is just good old American freedom at its best: the freedom of self-determination, the freedom to choose to practice as a person wants, the freedom of a businessperson to make good business choices. And medicine has become just another function of the market doing what markets claim to do best: distributing goods and services and leveraging the profit motive to create putative efficiencies.

Except. Except that it is not so simple. Because much of medicine and health care is a public process paid for with public money, medicine and health care should have a public purpose with meaningful public results. And there is plenty of evidence that our current medical services marketplace has failed miserably at improving the health and safety of Americans, during a period in which democracy also appears to be in eclipse.

One hundred years ago, most doctors in the United States were primary care doctors; only about 30 percent were specialists. Time, money, and culture changed that ratio, so now about 70 percent of US physicians are specialists and 30 percent are primary care physicians, as the business of medicine entrained the health care enterprise in this country. That's bad for us as a nation, because lots of evidence shows that health care systems with more primary care physicians have much lower costs (as much as 60 percent lower), longer life expectancy, and lower infant mortality—better public health overall.

The dearth of primary care physicians provides a great business opportunity for specialists. People without family doctors have little access to someone who can answer their questions about what ails them, so they take themselves to someone who they think might know the answer to those questions, even if that someone is quite expensive. Individuals who use specialists get stuck with much larger expenses than they would have if they saw their own doctor, because the specialty consultation costs more and because specialists are more likely to order expensive tests like CT scans, MRIs, or lab testing, often using equipment that the specialist partly or wholly owns. Communities where there are too few family doctors experience higher health care costs than they would if there were an adequate supply of primary care doctors and community health centers. Communities with too few primary care clinicians also see more people leave the community for health care, as specialists are usually located in cities or near hospitals. So less health care is provided in the community and by community residents, and wealth moves out of the community when specialists provide much—or most—of physician consultation.

Specialists believe that their high prices and big incomes are justified by the cost of a medical school education and by the years of training after medical school that specialty practice requires. (Primary care practice requires three years of post-graduate medical education; most specialists do four to seven years now.) But even those specialists who go into debt for medical school and think they paid for their own education accepted a much greater public contribution to their education and training than any of them wants to admit. Medical school tuition represents only about 3 percent of the cost of running a medical school. Most medical school income comes from their faculty practice plan, federally funded research, direct federal support, and contributions from hospitals, usually in the form of purchased services, as medical school faculty staff most university hospitals and hospitals buy the time of medical school faculty to support hospitals' clinical needs.[2]

It's not possible to know exactly how much of total medical school funding is public, in part because each medical school is different. Many state medical schools receive state funds to operate, while many private medical schools have significant endowments that help support the education of at least some of their students with grants and scholarships.

And even much of the indirect funding that medical schools receive from hospitals that purchase faculty clinical time is also public funding. The bulk of hospital physicians' payments, likely about 60 percent, are made by Medicaid and Medicare, and thus the bulk of medical schools' faculty-practice-plan income is publicly funded. (It might be argued that Medicare isn't exactly public funding, because the bulk of Medicare funds are contributed by each person in the form of salary deductions that employers have to match. True enough. But Medicare as a program was constructed by a public process in the public interest. And so it is entirely appropriate for Medicare to expend funds in the service of the public interest, which is exactly what it does when it funds graduate medical education.) The same is true of hospital income, only the federal participation is greater, likely 65 to 70 percent or more. Taken together, the greatest chunk of the cost of medical school education is funded by public money, likely 75 percent or more.

There's another way in which all medical students, specialists included, benefit from the resources of the communities in which they attend medical schools. Medical schools learn anatomy by dissecting cadavers. Those cadavers come from people who have donated their bodies to science, who allow their bodies to be dissected after they die so that young physicians can learn for the good of all. Few people, and too few physicians, think about or understand the value of this donation or even see it as a contribution, not to medical students themselves or even to medical schools, but a contribution to and for the good of the entire community. Medical education is a resource that comes from all of us. It cannot and should not be viewed as property to be controlled by the individuals who are educated in the process, but instead as community property that should be used for the good of all.

And that's just medical school. Residency training, the three to five or even seven years of training that is required before any physician can practice, is completely paid for by Medicare. No sleuthing was required to get that number. Every single dollar of resident salary and education expense is public money, via the Medicare trust fund, overseen and supervised by the Council on Graduate Medical Education, which is a division of HRSA, the Health Resources and Services Administration. During residency, specialists are paid $63,000 to $75,000 a year, with every single dollar (and more—hospitals get much more than salaries for running residency programs) paid by the US government via Medicare. Of course, physicians in training have to work hard. They work hard, they study constantly, they are under tremendous stress—but they are paid during the whole period by you and me. They don't own their resident training experience any more than police own their police cars or police stations.

And again, the community resources that are devoted to residency training are not just the Medicare money that pays for it. Poor and working people from around the nation use resident-run specialty clinics because those clinics are usually in teaching hospitals, which are usually located in densely populated urban communities. Poor and working people also use those resident-run specialty clinics because they have very limited access to specialty care: few specialists locate their offices in poor communities, many specialists don't accept the kind of insurance that poor and working people have (as described above), many don't accept Medicare, some don't accept Medicaid, and very few specialists indeed will provide care for people without insurance, especially those without the ability to pay $300 or $500 up front. That means that residents in training learn their specialties by "practicing"—literally and figuratively—on poor and working people. Poor and working people don't know they are part of a hidden social contract in which they "accept" care from resident physicians who are in the process of being trained and in return get specialty care to which they might not otherwise have access. (What an interesting social "contract," when one of the parties was never informed of the "deal" and so could never agree to it—a process that sounds like colonialism, paternalism, and coercion to me!)

In this way, part of the residency training that specialists and other physicians receive was "contributed" by the people they learned on, even though those people had no say whatsoever in their "contribution." So a good part of the training residents receive is a community resource, extracted from the community, and thus that training can't be said to be "owned" by the specialists who receive it any more than a fire truck can be said to be owned by the firefighters who drive it.

The de facto system in which poor people "allowed" themselves to be training fodder for specialists started to fray in the 1980s and completely collapsed by 2000. Medicine had been declared a business, not an ethical calling. Hospitals didn't see themselves as charitable institutions now, but as health care organizations competing with one another for health care dollars and hoping to expand their market share while improving their profitability. Specialists saw themselves as businesspeople working to maximize income, who often competed with hospitals for business in imaging centers and outpatient surgical facilities. By 2000, hospitals had run private primary care physicians off, replacing them with hospitalists to take care of those poor patients the hospitals couldn't find a way to "divert." Specialists usually still have to take calls for emergency patients who are admitted through the emergency department if they want operating-room privileges at a hospital, but most chafe at the need to do so.

Increasingly, hospitals employ specialists and pay them to cover the emergency room—and many hospitals work harder yet to "divert" poor and working people elsewhere.

In addition, most specialties work hard to keep the number of new specialists trained to a minimum, in order to maintain their monopoly on specialty care. The specialty boards work with the Council on Graduate Medical Education and with Medicare—Medicare!—to keep the numbers from growing. (Medicare worries, intelligently, that the more specialists there are, the higher the nation's costs will be, an observation supported by considerable evidence but one with the unintended side effect of increasing the monopoly power of specialists and specialty organizations.) Want to know why it takes three or four weeks to get in to see a neurologist or an orthopedist? Or six months to get an appointment with a new family doctor? Want to know why no psychiatrist accepts Medicare or Medicaid in your community? Blame Medicare. Blame Health and Human Services. And blame Congress. These shortages are created and maintained by your US federal government. Specialty supply is completely controlled by a public process, a process that is heavily influenced by the lobbying of self-interested specialty organizations. These dynamics feed into the supply of services and access to those services, with short supply being an effective way to drive prices—and specialty incomes—higher and higher. All facilitated, regulated, and paid for by your friendly Uncle Sam—US! We have met the enemy and again the enemy is US! Wealth extraction facilitated and orchestrated by state power once again.

What would specialty care in the United States look like if health care existed to strengthen communities rather than to drain them of resources?

First, if health care were for people and not for profit, we'd have double the number of primary care clinicians we have today and our need for specialists would be half of what it is now, because much of what specialists now do (like checking blood pressure and evaluating headaches) is actually primary care, and if there were enough primary care clinicians, that work would move back to primary care offices. So we'd suddenly have enough specialists instead of a shortage, and people would be able to get specialty care when they needed it and do so affordably, instead of waiting for weeks and having to stand at the sliding glass window where they take your information and your money and treat you like a number.

How is that again? How in the heck could we drop the demand for specialty care in half and lower the costs at the same time?

It's simple. In order to have health care that strengthens communities, we'd have to do what most advanced countries do: we'd have to have a health care system that provides primary care to every person in every neighborhood, town, and community. Yup, in order to improve specialty care, we'd start by providing primary care to all Americans. Likely less than 43 percent of Americans have and use primary care now.[3] Instead, most Americans go to hospital emergency departments—or directly to specialists—when they get sick. That fills ERs and specialist offices, runs up the cost of health care, and contributes to worsening public health outcomes. That's because, although ERs and specialists may be good at treating true emergencies and specialized medical problems, they aren't good at taking care of many of the real health problems most people report.

If we provided primary care to all Americans, the need for ERs, specialists, and hospital beds would be cut in half. That would free up specialists to care for people who really have the diseases and disorders in which they specialize. Lower demand would drop prices. If most specialists saw only patients with the diseases in which they specialize, the overtesting and overtreatment of the population would also shrink. Reduction of overtreatment would mean better health for individuals and lower costs for communities—and we might even be able to improve population health, if communities decided to spend those extra dollars on education, public housing, public transportation, public parks, and community development, which are the community services that produce far better health outcomes than spending on medical care.

Okay, but say the big fix—providing primary care to all Americans—is not on the horizon. Too much change for a nation that despairs of the status quo but hates to change even more. What can we do to make specialty care better at supporting communities? First, we should require that all clinicians see patients regardless of the ability to pay and that all accept Medicare and Medicaid as a requirement of licensure. All clinicians were trained with considerable public support. It is long past time for those clinicians to pay that public support forward and repay their functional debt to society.

We as a nation should increase the number of primary care and specialist clinicians, focusing on the recruitment of physicians from traditionally poor and underserved communities and from racial, language, and cultural minorities. We need clinicians who are connected to all our communities, and we need them to locate their practices in all our communities so that Americans are more equally served. Training specialists without training primary care clinicians is likely to increase the cost of health care, which is a burden on communities already, but training more clinicians might well reduce the disparities in access to specialty services that exist in communities today.

If we want to end the colonization of communities by specialty health care, we'll need to rethink medicine as a business and turn it back into an ethical enterprise by building a system of specialty care that serves all Americans, regardless of insurance or their ability to pay, as we develop the resources and organization needed to provide primary care to everyone in this country.

What does all this have to do with medical colonialism and wealth extraction? Well, if you own a fire truck, and you want to charge what the traffic will bear to put out fires, and there is no law against selling fire protection in a market economy, then the people who believe in the market will argue that you should be able to choose where to go to put out fires and what to charge and whose fires to put out.

But what if you don't own the fire truck? What if the community owns the fire truck and you are only borrowing it? What if you hijacked a fire truck from another place and drove it here?

The health care enterprise is a public process at its core. Health care, some health care, is a service that all of us are likely to need at some point in our lives, and the prevention part of health care is something that most of us—and all communities—benefit from. The public health process, which tracks diseases and conditions that impact communities, is a process all of us benefit from as well, because it lets us minimize our risks. Most health care in the US is publicly funded. To paraphrase Michael Pollan, we need some health care, not too much, mostly primary care—but we need hospitals and specialists sometimes, and when we do need them, we need them badly. My specialist and hospital colleagues have hijacked the fire truck that we all paid for together, and now they want us to pay them through the nose when there is a fire.

It's time to take the fire truck back.

CHAPTER FIVE

Administrators, Consultants, Lawyers, and Doctors

Back in 1960, before the health care industrial complex had grown so huge, we spent about 5 percent of our gross national product on health care, or about $26 billion—or $146 per person per year. That's about $1,353 per person, adjusted for inflation.[1] We now spend more than 18 percent of the GNP, or close to $4 trillion a year—about $12,000 per person per year. During this period, government's share of health care spending went from 23 percent of all spending to 43 percent, while businesses' share went from 14 to 21 percent and household share fell from 56 to 28 percent (in 2013).[2] If it makes you feel better that so much less of that money, on a percentage basis, is coming out of your pocket, think again: In inflation-adjusted dollars, in 1960 the average person was spending 56 percent of $1,353 (in 2021 dollars), or $757. In 2021, you will likely spend 28 percent of $12,000, or $3,360, so each person's *inflation-adjusted* out-of-pocket health care spending more than quadrupled in fifty years—the average person spends more than four times as much of their pocket money on health care! And to make matters worse, the government and the business shares of spending didn't come from nowhere. They came from the pocket of each and every one of us as well: the government's share from taxes and the businesses' share from money that could have been used to increase wages. During this period, US life expectancy grew from sixty-nine years to seventy-eight years—but the evidence showing that this increase was due to medical care is weak at best. Many epidemiologists believe that the increase was due to other factors: Better education. Better traffic safety. Better income. Better housing. Fewer deaths in warfare, at least for Americans.

But all those increases in health care cost? Where do they come from? There are lots of explanations for those cost increases, to be sure. Ewe Reinhart, the great Princeton health economist, thought prices of medical services, particularly doctor's charges, contributed tremendously to our health care costs, especially when those costs are compared to costs in other nations. But many others have described the huge influx of "strangers at the bedside," the crowd of people—administrators, clerks, lawyers, information technologists, computer hardware people and network people, billers, software designers and electronic-medical-record trainers, billing coders, quality assurance people, compliance people—who are involved in the huge US health bureaucracy.[3] Where there is a will, there are relatives. Where there is health care spending, there are folks in suits and ties ready to make health care infinitely more complex and charge billions along the way.

In 1960, there was a lone family doctor in many communities, and maybe he (it was usually *he*, then) worked with a nurse and maybe even a receptionist (almost always *she*, then and now). Now every family doctor is supported by at least four other people, and that's in a primary care practice. Many specialists have a whole army to support them.

In 1960, there were no health care policy lawyers; no compliance officers to do the work that the health care policy lawyers dream up; no quality assurance officers to do the work that insurance companies, Medicare, and Medicaid dream up; no billers and receipts payable clerks; no pharmacy benefits managers and no practice administrators; few insurance company executives; and few hospital administrators—the list goes on and on. When one person has a health care dollar, it looks like a whole tribe of people show up to grab that dollar—and then they forget to make change!

When I worked in a community health center between 2015 and 2020, I saw how administrative colonialism works. That health center was in one of the poorest parts of Rhode Island, in Central Falls, a city that is about 80 percent minority. Most of the medical assistants and receptionists were people of color. Perhaps 20 percent of the nursing and medical staff were people of color. But there was not one person from the community the health center served who worked in the senior administration (including me!). The "C" suite was entirely white and entirely composed of people who lived in the suburbs. They made all the operating decisions. And they took all the income from the larger salary lines and moved it to the suburbs with them, to help fund their boats and campers. (I was in that group for a while, but I generated my salary through patient care revenue and grants; I was never convinced, though, that what I was doing was ethical either, so I ended up donating a fair amount of what I earned back to the community we served.)

The health policy world—the academics and bureaucrats who study, discuss, and talk about how to organize health care in the United States—noticed some time ago that the administrative cost of health care in the US has mushroomed over the last thirty years. In 2017, for example, US insurers and providers spent $812 billion on administration, or about $2,497 per capita and 34.2 percent of national health expenditures.[4] Administrative costs as a percentage of all health care spending has more than doubled since 1970.[5] By 2016, there were twenty-two times more nonphysician and nondentist employees in health care settings as there were physicians and dentists. As stated in the JAMA Forum, "About 17% of these employees were registered nurses (RNs), 46% were other health care workers (technicians, home health aides, nursing aides, and others), and *37% were nonmedical workers (such as business managers and office assistants)*."[6] More than one-third of all people involved in health care are now administrative workers, not health care workers.

Some people regard this spending as the price we must pay for maintaining consumer choice in health care, although how all this overhead is supposed to improve choice is unclear, particularly because with limited networks and vertically integrated health care systems, most of us now have less choice than ever, not more.[7] But viewed another way, health care administrative cost represents wealth transfer, away from individuals and communities and into the pockets of those administrative workers, who might otherwise be unemployed. Even more, the administrative cadre represents the misappropriation of democracy inside health care. Now patients and their doctors aren't free to make their own decisions about what they want and what makes sense for each person and community. Instead, there are layers and layers of bureaucrats administering pages upon pages of rules, laying out what patients can have and what clinicians can say and do. Now most clinicians work late into the night, checking off boxes on computer screens those administrators thought up for them to check, administrators who have never cared for a patient and have no understanding whatsoever of, or concern for, the public's health. A senior leader of that community health center I worked for, when I tried to expand a novel, exciting, and very successful smoking-cessation program we'd started, said, "Smoking cessation? We don't get paid for smoking cessation. We only get paid to see patients. We can't do anything like that!" We might need to nuance our definition of colonialism somewhat and call this *administrative colonialism*, a process whereby people who have no training or expertise in an area of endeavor invade medicine, using the administrative state as a cover, and take its resources for themselves.

During the COVID-19 pandemic, I worked as the chief health strategist for the City of Central Falls, Rhode Island. During that period, I had the occasion to be on lots of Zoom calls with political and public health people who worked together to address the outbreak, a situation I discussed in this book's introduction in detail. On every call, there would be several people, sometimes one but usually three or five or more, who I didn't recognize. I'd ask on the call or after and find out again and again that these people worked for consulting groups paid for by the state: the

Boston Consulting Group, Alvarez & Marsal, Deloitte, John Snow, Inc., and others had people at our virtual table. In little Rhode Island alone, we spent $12.4 million just on Alvarez & Marsal in 2020.[8] Often the consultants on the Zoom call were young and sure of themselves and were coming to us from Missouri or Illinois or Minnesota—and didn't actually know anything about public health. Most had no public health training or experience whatsoever, and none had health professional training. They were nice enough, but they knew nothing about Central Falls, which is 70 percent Latino, about 10 percent Black, and has large Cape Verdean and Liberian communities. None of the consultants spoke Spanish or Cape Verdean Creole—most had never heard of Cape Verde and didn't know what Creole was—but they were in a big hurry to tell us how to organize our COVID-19 response, and very well paid to do so. When I asked why we were using so many consultants, people looked at me like I was from Mars. "It's all federal dollars," I was told. "Don't worry about it." As if federal dollars don't come from the tax dollars every community pays every single year.

One problem was that the consultants didn't appear to know what they were talking about and weren't basing their "advice" on good evidence or long experience. A second problem was that this federal money wasn't being spent on the community itself, hiring bi- or trilingual community people who were put out of work by the pandemic. The third problem is the way these national consulting groups, who are enriched in this process, use their money to create a Beltway revolving door—you work for one of these groups when you are out of government during a political change but maintain contacts with your former colleagues, and then you return to government or industry when the administration changes—to lobby for yet more money for themselves. Again, people with something to sell co-opt state power to enrich themselves as they expropriate resources that communities need to make life better for the people who live in the communities from which all this money actually comes.

In June 2021, I spent seven hours in a Zoom meeting giving a deposition about the epidemic of opiate overdose deaths nationally and in Rhode Island, part of a process by which states were suing pharmaceutical companies, wholesalers, and retailers for damages, asserting those damages had been caused by those corporations' alleged negligence. I had been right in the middle of that epidemic in 2012 and 2013 as director of the Rhode Island Department of Health when the opiate overdose epidemic worsened, and I had worked hard as part of state government to stop the flow of opiates in every way we could. I noticed during the meeting that there was one of me, an unpaid witness compelled to be there by the court, talking to six different lawyers, all paid, as well as a stenographer and a video and Zoom producer, paid as well. I'm guessing that those lawyers bill $500 an hour or more. So my little deposition likely cost someone $3,000 an hour, or over $20,000. None of the people in the meeting live, work, or shop in the communities most impacted by the epidemic. One might argue that this legal process is a normal cost of doing business, an argument that seems completely correct. Except. Except that when one person has a dollar they didn't work for, some other person worked for a dollar they didn't get. The costs of all this activity are passed, invisibly, to working people and to poor communities, who pay for all this and much more out of limited funds that could and should be used to make those communities stronger and more resilient.

To some degree, you can't see or even argue with all this "little stuff"—all the extra costs, the lawyers, the judges, the court reporters, and also the accountants and actuaries who will figure out how much money is involved, what might be called administrative overhead. But all this "little stuff" adds up. Lawyers and judges et al., many of whom mean well, contribute sometimes unknowingly to the fleecing of communities and the progressive centralization of wealth by allowing the health care market to continue along the road it is going, making the rich richer and the poor poorer and weakening our democracy in the process.

Lawyers who are part of the malpractice bar, suing or defending doctors and hospitals, are a relatively small (given the total cost of health care) but significant contributor to health care costs. The cost of malpractice litigation in 2008 was estimated to represent about $55.6 billion, or 2.4 percent of the expense of health care—and if that percentage has remained the same, it likely represents about $96 billion in total costs today, with about a third of the overall costs, or about $32 billion per year, going to attorney's fees.[9]

Doctors as a class are no better, and perhaps worse, if you think that we have an ethical obligation to use our knowledge and moral authority to lead the nation out of this morass. Doctors are trained to think about epidemiology and public health. We are trained to read the studies that have been telling us, over and over, for the last fifty years, that income inequality is bad for health, that health care spending on hospitals and specialists worsens the public health, and that other countries that have organized not-for-profit health care systems have far better health outcomes at far lower prices. And, as I described in the chapter on specialists, physicians are trained primarily at public expense, although few of us understand that. So not only do we take money out of the poor communities and move that money to rich suburbs, not only have we squandered the public's trust by failing to fix the health care mess while using the training the public paid us to receive, but we also have a profound golden handcuff problem: we don't move ourselves to lead as we have been trained to do because we are too well paid, are too comfortable, and aren't willing to jeopardize our incomes in the service of the ideals we claimed when we entered medicine as a profession.

Lawyers promise society nothing when they become lawyers, other than to uphold the law and defend the right to a fair trial. Consultants are only hired guns. They may aspire to use their skills in the public interest, but those aspirations are belied by their hefty incomes at the public's expense. But doctors commit to unself-interested advocacy, to putting the needs of patients before our own needs. When we use our (mostly publicly funded) training in any other way, when we use the public's trust in the service of our own incomes, we are perpetuating a most cruel colonialism, in which we exploit public trust instead of military might to extract resources from communities—and use that expropriated public trust to enrich ourselves.

CHAPTER SIX

Primary Care

For about seventeen years, from 1991 until 2008, I lived in little Scituate, Rhode Island, where I practiced family medicine, and for about eleven of those seventeen years, I practiced out of the basement of my house. It was an older style of primary care, a style that started to die out by the 1960s and was almost completely gone by 2000. Once upon a time, when we had local banks that lent money to local people who wanted to buy a house or a business, when we had local pharmacies that might open at night to dispense a prescription to someone seriously ill, when we had local newsstands and local newspapers, we also had family doctors who lived in the communities they served and who employed local people to work in those practices. A few local people. Usually very few. Maybe one or two, back in the days before Medicare and its bureaucracy, Medicaid and its bureaucracy, health insurance and its bureaucracy. Way back in history, before electronic medical records and doctors who looked at screens instead of you (so, before 2009)—because way back in history, family doctors didn't need so many people working for them, since the practice of medicine in general, and the practice of medical billing in particular, was so much simpler. Family doctors didn't generate lots of economic activity, so we didn't take much money out of communities, and because we tended to live in or near the communities we served, we supported each community economically as well as with health care services, once upon a time.

Now I have several colleagues who practice primary care in community health centers in one community. And drive off at night in their Teslas to gated communities or to wealthy enclaves—and send their children to private schools. That's one kind of colonialism to be sure, what might be called primary care colonialism. But that behavior, increasingly common, doesn't exhaust the way primary care and colonialism intersect.

Now, of course, even primary care has become a huge economic engine, one that creates cash flow and generates profits. Now there are a number of primary care corporations that are funded by venture capital, private equity, and hedge funds and that are traded on major stock exchanges and have market capitalizations of a billion dollars or more: Oak Street Health, $14 billion; ChenMed, $7.4 billion; 1Life Healthcare, $4.75 billion, which just bought Iora Health for $2.3 billion. (The clinic chain 1Life Healthcare, which became One Medical, was acquired by Amazon in July of 2022 for $4 billion.) CVS bought MinuteClinic in 2006 for an estimated $160 million, but it's hard to know how much of CVS's $109 billion market cap is due to MinuteClinic, how much is from its five-thousand-plus retail pharmacies, and how much is from its pharmaceutical benefits management and other businesses. And there are four or five other retail pharmacy-based clinic chains that have significant value, value based on the resources those clinics mine in every community in the US. Those resources often leave their communities as profit—although they do leave behind the salaries of clerks, receptionists, nurse-practitioners, and sometimes pharmacists and primary care physicians, depending on the business model of each particular operation.[1]

You wouldn't think who supplies primary care services would matter very much: a throat culture is a throat culture, regardless of who obtains it, and an antibiotic for a urinary tract infection is an antibiotic, and a flu shot is a flu shot. Except it does matter, and it matters tremendously both for the public health and for the dense web of relationships that holds families and communities together.

I've talked up to this point about medical colonialism as a process that denudes communities of financial resources, and that is a significant issue. But when we look at primary care, we see medical colonialism in a new light: as a process that denudes communities of the rich fabric of relationships that communities need to sustain themselves, and even of the interactive process that we understand to be democracy. Colonialism takes more than money from a place. It removes relationships that are worth far more than money at the end of the day. History and identity reside in those relationships, which are necessary if each community is to see itself as a valuable and meaningful place to live, a place with a unique identity and a reason for its people to be connected to one another into the future.

Here's what happened when retail pharmacy-based clinics got into the retail clinic "business."

By 2009, all pharmacies became able to give flu shots, a process that had started about ten years before, when retail chains expanded and decided to get into the flu shot business. The number of places in the United States where people could get flu shots doubled, to about 120,000. But the flu vaccination rate stayed the same, at about 37 percent of the population. Also during this period, marketing and the Internet began to convince people that they didn't need family doctors, that they could go online and figure most things out for themselves or, if they needed something, could hustle on over to the local MinuteClinic and, in the parlance of marketers, "get their needs met." During this period, the number of people eighteen to twenty-nine who had and used a family doctor dropped to less than 55 percent.[2] (Truth be told, that percentage had been dropping for years, in part because of the Internet and retail-based clinics, but also because family doctors were so slow to adapt to the needs of the communities they served—with few evening hours, no telephone availability, little email availability, and long waits for appointments—and because of a relative shortage of family doctors.)

When the COVID-19 vaccine became available, retail-based clinics and large community health centers—and not primary care doctors—began to give shots, and the immunization rate quickly got stuck at between 60 and 70 percent in the states where immunization hadn't become the source of ideological warfare.

Why? Well, people used to rely on a family doctor to prompt them to get flu shots and to make things like the COVID-19 shot feel safe, but now family doctors are going away—most people don't have one. The income from giving flu shots, which represented about 10 percent of the yearly income of many family doctors, had shifted from the office of the family doctor to the retail pharmacy. Before long, the work of ordering flu shots (which had become its own little market fiasco with its own spot market and set of futures, like the market for hogs or corn) and of reminding people to get flu shots had too little return on investment, and soon most family doctors stopped giving flu shots altogether, because the work of doing that—of obtaining vaccines and calling people in to get shots—was suddenly not worth the trouble. Part of the financial support of primary care practice went away. There was less reason for existing practices to hire new doctors, less financial health in each independent practice, and, before long, fewer practices in communities.

But look at what was also lost in the process. When family doctors gave flu shots, they also checked in with their patients, reminding them about checkups, cholesterol tests, mammograms, and the like. They bugged the people who are most vulnerable to get sick from the flu—the elderly and the infirm—to get their flu shots, and they kept bugging these people, and the rest of their patients and communities, to do so. Each time a primary care practice calls or touches a person, the relationship between doctor and patient deepens. Each touch provides the opportunity for many things: for prevention, but also for deepening trust and connection. Some of that was lost when primary care doctors gave up on flu shots.

Even so, even I was surprised that when COVID-19 hit, government itself gave up on primary care doctors and went directly to Big Pharma, retail-based pharmacies, the National Guard, and a host of consultants to get people immunized. In Rhode Island, primary care doctors weren't even in the first or second group of people to be immunized themselves. They weren't immunized until late January 2021, and only after a number of people, me included, raised the alarm. In most of the United States, primary care doctors and practices weren't asked to immunize their own patients at all until late in the pandemic. They weren't asked or paid to make lists of their patients over eighty and then over sixty-five and with severe chronic disease, the people who were at most risk of hospitalization and death and who should have been immunized first, and they weren't charged with the responsibility of calling those patients in and putting shots in all those arms. That meant that these doctors, nurse-practitioners, PAs, and their practices, the people in health care most trusted by their patients, were not asked to counsel patients about the vaccine, were not asked to explain the science behind it, and were not asked to answer people's questions. Is there any doubt why we saw so many people in the US afraid to get a vaccine? The "system" had walked right around the health professionals many people trusted and acted like that trust didn't matter, that all that mattered was "orders" coming from Washington and state capitals—orders and mandates instead of relationships, questions, answers, and information about public health and science, which could have and should have been delivered person by person, retail not wholesale, by people who Americans knew and trusted and who knew and trusted and loved them back.

By not using primary care practices, we both failed to vaccinate the population against COVID-19 quickly and lost the opportunity for primary care clinicians to connect with their patients one more time, to address other health issues, and to prevent some disease—and to update and strengthen the relationship between doctor and patient.

By devaluing primary care, we've also lost relationships that have value in themselves.

In 1991, when I was new in practice, I inherited an old country practice in tiny Foster, Rhode Island, where people were used to waiting two hours to see the doctor. *We can't have people wait,* I said to myself. *People have busy lives. They should expect to be seen on time. That shows respect. We need to modernize.* So I changed our hours and our scheduling, and pretty soon we got the wait down to fifteen minutes.

To my surprise, instead of patients being happy and congratulating the practice on our great achievement, people became quite angry. Why? People in that little rural town *liked* waiting for two hours. They *liked* seeing their neighbors and friends in the waiting room and catching up a little. And now the waiting room was empty.

Instead of working with primary care doctors, the COVID-19 response weakened the primary care delivery system at precisely the moment it desperately needed to be strengthened. Government did that. State power was used to shift the locus of care from communities to national corporations, away from local health professionals with a duty to provide unself-interested advocacy and put the needs of the patient first and toward for-profit businesses. Pharma et al. didn't need gunboats. They had a virus and lobbyists and a compliant government, and they rode that virus hard, to the tune of billions, perhaps trillions, of dollars.

Once upon a time, family doctors helped build community. The medical marketplace hasn't been able to carry off relationships as if they were raw material, because relationships aren't commodities. But the medical marketplace has distorted and destroyed the context and continuity of relationships, as if medicine and health care were an iron mine or a copper mine in a developing nation, as if the streams around that iron or copper mine had all been polluted by the process of extracting the ore, as if the polluted streams killed off the forests around the mine and made farming impossible—well, you get the picture.

Colonialism isn't just toxic because of the way it exploits the resources of a place, carrying them off. Colonialism is also toxic because of how it destroys the culture and environment of the colonized place, leaving behind a battered earth and battered communities when the colonialists sail away home.

Colonialism? Wealth extraction? Doesn't matter what you call it. The corporate practice of health care—the injection of the market into the intimate life of a community—disrupts the life of that community, forever weakening it.

CHAPTER SEVEN

Insurance Companies

In a certain way and once upon a time, health insurance companies represented real community assets. Once upon a time, there wasn't much medicine could do for a person other than set broken bones and take care of people after heart attacks. People went to the doctor when they were sick, and going to the doctor was something most people could afford.

As medicine developed technologically and became a market enterprise, those dynamics changed. People developed dread diseases that had names and if not cures, at least treatments. Hospitals became huge and expensive financial enterprises. If you got into a bad accident or needed major surgery, the costs of hospitalization and surgery could swamp the financial security of all but a few Americans. Health insurance companies, which generally started out as nonprofits, were created as collaborative enterprises in which people came together to pool their resources in case of a rare event, a medical disaster that threatened to cause a personal financial catastrophe.

Beginning in the 1850s, many immigrant communities and early labor unions had sickness funds, to which everyone contributed small weekly or monthly amounts, and thus were able to support their members through periods of illness or disability. Workers' compensation insurance began about 1912, created by employers to defend themselves financially after the courts determined that they could be held responsible for injuries on the job. Most insurance companies got their start in 1929, at the beginning of the Great Depression, when Baylor

University Hospital in Dallas began providing up to twenty-one days of hospital care to schoolteachers for six dollars per person per year. Other groups soon adopted similar plans, and other hospitals around the country quickly adopted this model: the hospitals did this to fund their operations during the Depression, and the employers and communities jumped in to protect the financial security of their members and employees during hard times.

By 1932, there were hundreds of these plans in hundreds of localities, and the American Hospital Association began the process of accrediting them, insisting that they remain nonprofit, emphasize the public welfare, not compete with one another (!), use "dignified" promotion, and ensure the free choice of physician. How far we have come from those founding principles! The first of these plans was enabled and regulated by New York State in 1934, and by 1939, twenty-five states had passed enabling legislation for what was now called Blue Cross, which quickly created its own national coordinating organization and employed its own lobbyists. Membership exploded in the 1940s, during a period of wage and price controls just after World War II, when employers couldn't attract or hold employees by offering better pay. Instead, they hoped to attract and hold new employees by offering better benefits, in particular by adding one benefit that was widely sought after: hospitalization insurance. By 1949, Blue Cross had nineteen million members across the nation.[1] Private health insurance, made up of health insurance companies that were not charted by the state and were not nonprofits like Blue Cross, also started in the 1930s; it grew in parallel with the Blue Cross plans and had about seventeen million subscribers by 1949.

What started as a local phenomenon, community by community, grew quickly into a big business, promoted by people and organizations that had something to gain. Health insurers were often statewide organizations chartered (as nonprofits) by state legislatures—and thus state sanctioned, with implicit state power behind them.

Note that the insurance process itself is always extractive when it operates on a statewide or national scale. When the economic enterprise of health care exists without third-party payment, that economic exchange is always local: you pay directly for the service you receive where you receive it, and the provider of the service benefits economically, with no one else involved. Third-party payers and their legions of claims processors, however, are almost always elsewhere, and they use their market power to skim off some of the funding to run their own operations, to pay their executives, and to create profit. The Affordable Care Act of 2010 was remarkable in many ways, but part of its innovation was to require a "medical loss ratio" for some insurers of at least 80 percent. That's bureaucracy-speak for restricting the cream that insurers could skim off the top to 20 percent of premium. That's right. Many insurers were taking more: 20, 30, even 50 percent of premium was being used for salaries, overhead, and profit in the same period that only 5 percent of premium was being spent on primary care, which provided 50 percent of the medical services on any given day!

Third-party payers consolidate capital and information. They use market forces to pay a lower price for services and demand a higher price for premiums. That gives them the ability to extract a significant proportion of the cash flow, which they keep for themselves—money that would have changed hands locally and stayed local if the state hadn't intervened to enable this wealth extraction process. Nice work, as they say, if you can get it. The consolidated business practices of insurers are not dependent on place. Insurers put their offices wherever it is least expensive and more convenient for their senior executives and often move their call centers offshore, to developing nations where they can pay low salaries.

Health insurers will likely argue that their processes have created a more efficient marketplace, allowed more people to get insurance, and achieved better health outcomes as a result. But a generation or two of public health data says that just ain't so. Take a moment to follow the money when it comes to health insurance. During the years 1940 to 2020, more people having health insurance in the United States was associated with more health care expenditure overall—and less money in the hands of individuals and communities. This was a period in which money and jobs flowed out of small communities and into big cities around the nation and the world—an era at the end of which the average life expectancy of Americans fell, income and wealth inequality deepened, and democracy struggled to stay afloat both here and around the world. Most of those changes were due to factors beyond health insurance, but the health care piece, which caused more people to spend more money on health care, was facilitated by health insurance, and the health insurance process aided and abetted the concentration of wealth that was part and parcel of these changes.

Beginning in 1997, insurance company executives used their growing money and power to get the rules changed so that the state could charter nonprofit entities to become for-profits with huge market capitalizations.[2] Individual state Blue Cross and Blue Shield companies, the state-chartered nonprofits, merged and quickly morphed into national companies that were for-profit. A few nonprofit companies remain—Blue Cross Blue Shield of Massachusetts, Texas, Rhode Island, and a number of other states—but those are now the exception, not the rule. (A number of other nonprofit health insurance companies, such as Kaiser Permanente, Harvard Pilgrim, and Neighborhood Health Plan of both Massachusetts and Rhode Island, continue to exist and compete in the marketplace, but many observers think their operations are barely distinguishable from the operations of for-profit insurers.) What had been an exercise in community self-protection morphed, between 1997 and 2015, into financial behemoths that profit from the fears and misfortunes of millions of people. Meet the new boss. Same as the old boss. Now people are afraid to go without insurance. But they also can't afford the insurance that is available.

In 2009, the government got into the act again. Convinced by highly paid pundits that it is health insurance—and not *some medical care, occasionally*—that saves lives, or more precisely that the lack of health insurance increases the risk of death, your US federal government, via the Affordable Care Act, began to require that people have health insurance or pay a penalty. Kind of dizzying when you view the history this way. What had been created by people in communities acting together to protect one another became a state-required—not sanctioned, but *required*—resource shift, a tax. The intentions behind making insurance required were for the most part honorable, but notice how in the space of less than one hundred years, the marketplace process had captured a community function and turned it around so that it was now a weapon of colonialist expansion. An explorer had gone out, found a beautiful island where people were living in peace as hunter-gathers, sailed home, and reported on what he had found, and then his mother country sent warships with guns firing and trumpets blaring to force the inhabitants into submission. Wow!

Note here that Medicare and Medicaid, which both got started in 1965, are nothing but state-owned insurance companies: Medicare is the insurer for people over sixty-five, owned by the federal government. Medicaid was the state-level insurer for people living in poverty, at first, and then became the insurer for children and pregnant women, and then the insurer for more and more lower-income people (as more and more people became lower income with progressive income inequality in the United States).

At first, it appeared that these publicly owned entities could not be bought. But then, with the passage of time, entrepreneurs in the private market figured out how to crack them open: Medicare can be manipulated by going to Congress and by manipulating reimbursement rates and coverage for various procedures, services, and products. (Remember all those very nice motorized scooters that people with disabilities now have and are advertised on TV? They are just the most visible example of how this works, but it usually works for drugs that cost fifty to a hundred thousand dollars a year, or surgical procedures that cost tens of thousands, or hospital bed days, which each cost more for one day than most Americans make in a month.)

The private insurance market, for example, talked Congress into something called Medicare Advantage. They said, "Give us what you are paying out for Medicare per person per month, only less 15 percent, and we'll provide all the care those people need. You'll save money, and we'll profit by organizing and managing the medical care of those people more efficiently." Seemed like a good deal at first. But then somehow, over time, that "We'll take 15 percent *less*" became "We'll take 15 percent *more*," and since the per-person cost of Medicare is something like $12,000 per person per year (in 2020), they are making out like bandits, to the tune of at least $1,800 per person per year, pretty much just for signing a contract with Medicare. (Okay. It's way more complicated than that. The insurance companies have to jump through all sorts of bureaucratic hoops to get your money. But they get it. And most of the time they didn't do one thing to earn it.)

There's a similar story in Medicaid, which is funded and administered differently. Generally, 50 percent of the funds came from the federal government and 50 percent came from states' governments, and the states ran their own little insurance companies with these funds, only they really weren't so little, usually insuring something like 15 percent of most states' populations by 2015—and most states didn't run their Medicaid programs well. States didn't run Medicaid well at all, in part because people with money used their influence on the state legislatures to sway policy decisions, so the who-got-paid and what-they-got-paid in each state was often a function of political clout and not a result of evidence that showed the public health benefit of each choice. So hospitals, which have the most political clout but the least public health value, usually got paid quite well, while primary care clinicians, who have the most public health value but the least clout, were poorly paid indeed under Medicaid in most states.

Insurance companies then came to states and said, "Pay us a certain amount per month and we'll run Medicaid for you, and very much like Medicare Advantage." The states said sure, and the insurance companies had themselves another per-person per-month bonanza. Doctors and hospitals do the work. Insurance companies pocket much of the money. The tax money that is raised in each state now goes into private pockets. Much of that money is sucked off to other places and so does not circulate in that state, and everyone in each state is poorer as a result, except for the rich guys, who own stock in the insurance companies, hospital holding companies, pharma and medical equipment companies, and the venture capital, private equity, and hedge fund firms, which now own the land and the physical plant of what used to be public hospitals, who all make out like bandits in this scenario.

How much money? Federal Medicaid regulations require that commercial insurance plans spend at least 85 percent of the money the government pays them for medical services, which means they get to keep 15 percent, the same percentage that insurers who offer Medicare Advantage plans receive over and above the cost of Medicare itself.[3] Because Medic*aid* spending is less than Medic*are* spending, per member per year, insurance companies offering Medicaid managed-care plans make less money. But Medicaid managed-care spending averaged about $5,500 per recipient per year in 2018, so the insurance companies likely net about $800 per person per year.[4] For 15 percent of the US population! Compare that to the cost of primary care, which is about $500 to $600 per person per year.[5] The insurance companies make more than the primary care clinicians who deliver the care make. And their CEOs don't have to go to medical school. Or answer the phone at three a.m. to talk to the mother of a sick child.

Put another way, insurance companies earn $800 per person per year for the work that primary care clinicians do, for which those clinicians are paid $500 per person per year, in a process created, regulated, and supervised by the state, which also licenses the primary care clinicians and requires certain behaviors and practices of those clinicians. Insurance companies move that money out of state. Primary care clinicians live in the state, work there, go to the dentist there, eat in the restaurants there, and go to the hairdresser and the barber there, at least as long as those haven't been shut down by COVID-19.

You might as well have gunships in the harbors demanding tribute. We've prettied up our gunships. Clinicians work all their professional lives hoping to care for and strengthen their communities—or at least they once did. Once, they were part of the communities they served. But now they serve other masters, and the value of their labor is cash to be carried away by others, as they have become unwitting accomplices to these transactions, enablers of this theft of resources.

But the essential dynamics—a market for services focused on profit, fueled by wealth extracted using the power of the state—is exactly the same as when the United States trained a little invasion force in 1954 and sent it into Guatemala to topple a democratically elected government so that United Fruit could continue exporting bananas at low cost.

Not all of what health insurers do is government supervised. Some 60 percent of us have commercial insurance and not a government program. Or no insurance at all. In order to understand health insurance and its role in health care in the US, you also need to understand the legal umbrella that health insurance in the US operated under. The McCarran-Ferguson Act of 1954 made the "business of insurance," including the business of health insurance (along with, amazingly, Major League Baseball), immune from federal antitrust laws until other legislation passed in 2021 removed that immunity. That allowed health insurers to share information about customers and suppliers, which effectively let insurers collude on pricing and policies. This collusion, which went hand in hand with the market's power imbalance between hospitals and other health care market actors, led to the further concentration of wealth in the hands of insurers and hospitals: hospitals used their political and market power to push up prices while insurers could learn what their competitors were paying for services and were charging, so commercial insurers didn't have to compete aggressively on price.

The McCarran-Ferguson Act created one more way for the medical-industrial complex to fleece communities. Hospitals got paid what they asked. Insurers could charge what they wanted without effective competition. Employers who bought health insurance for their employees had little choice in the matter, since all insurers charged about the same, and the only people who got hurt were . . . the people and communities who paid the bills, i.e., you and me. Communities carried a huge burden of this cost because large numbers of municipal employees—teachers, firefighters, and police—have health insurance guaranteed them as part of their contracts. That meant that communities all over America cut services—firehouses and many extracurricular activities for schools, community centers and swimming pools in the summer, adult education and the support of libraries—all in order to support the growing cost of health insurance, which rose 4 to 10 percent a year for thirty years, at twice the rate of inflation. Guess why taxes in local communities all over the nation keep going up? Price and wage inflation created the need for more tax *dollars*. But the inflation of health insurance costs, usually twice the rate of price and wage inflation, required increased tax *rates*.

While no one was looking, health insurance became the vehicle hospitals and other health system market players used to transfer the wealth of communities into the pockets of first insurers and then, through Big Pharma, venture capital and private equity firms, hedge funds, hospitals, medical equipment companies, and finally investors, as all these market players used the public process to transform health insurers from community enterprises we all owned to for-profit businesses owned by investors. All hidden in plain sight.

What's most disturbing is the complicity of both government and health professionals, both of whom had a legal and ethical obligation to advocate for the people they served and both of whom failed in that obligation.

What's even more sad is that the colonized people and communities weren't on some continent far away and out of sight. The colonized people were our fellow citizens and our communities, which were cannibalized by those of us who put their personal gain before the public good.

Is there a role for health insurance in a nation with a health care system that exists to improve the public's health? Maybe, but it is a tiny role at best, one that doesn't matter much. Health insurance companies are good at two things: they are good actuaries, and they are good at studying data on cost and outcomes and choosing the best providers of highly specialized but rarely used services. Actuaries study populations of people and use pooled data to predict how long people will live and what kind of resources people will consume as they live and die, and they then predict the costs of individuals' lives based on what is known about the personal health risks of those individuals. That kind of work happens all the time at Medicare and Medicaid and is useful for resource planning. In a nation with a health care system that cares for everyone, most health-care-related actuarial work will move into government, but there is still plenty of work for actuaries at life insurance companies and concerns that sell annuities and other retirement-related financial products.

There is also no reason that health insurance companies wouldn't continue to exist and offer insurance for people who want private medical care or insurance for the luxury side of health care—cosmetic surgery, for example, or fancy rooms in public hospitals. The people who now do marketing for insurance companies and those who study providers of services could help the remaining insurance companies decide which providers to work with and negotiate what to pay them.

That, of course, assumes a world in which people trust government enough to allow it to create a public not-for-profit health care *system*, supplying health care services and paying for them directly. That's a world in which government—mostly state and local government—figures out how to do all those things and more with effectiveness and integrity. Should such a world magically come into being, of course, we'd need to plan for the re-education and new employment of the millions of people who now work for health insurance companies, and many other millions as well—about seven million in all, the one-third of the twenty-two million health care workers who do work that is unnecessary but that exists to support the health insurance process.

This analysis of the transition away from an insurance-fueled health services system and toward a public not-for-profit health care system, one that is focused on improving and maintaining the public's health, tells us something critical about health care and health care reform in the United States. We've just learned that health care and what purports to be a crisis, most of the time, along with all the Sturm und Drang about changing public policy concerning health care, isn't about health care at all. Our angst and our challenge are about *government* and about making government effective and reliable.

We are wasting more than a trillion and a half dollars a year, and many lives, because we haven't figured out how to make government work. We can't trust government to perform one of its essential functions, which is to deliver an essential service that every American needs to keep this democracy functioning. So we contract that service out to the market, and the market does exactly what it is designed to do, which is maximize profit. We can either grow up and learn to govern ourselves, or we will pay through the nose for a health care system we didn't get and for population health that is second- or third-rate at best. As we watch democracy wither and die.

CHAPTER EIGHT

Research

I n the fall of 2020, I got a telephone call from a very ethical colleague who is an infectious disease specialist and a vaccine researcher. She'd been asked to recruit subjects for one of the COVID-19 vaccine trials that would be conducted locally and wanted my help recruiting subjects who were from Central Falls, Rhode Island, the small, mostly Latino city in which I worked. Research subjects from different cultural and language communities would allow more accurate study of the vaccine, because we'd be able to prove that it worked—or didn't—for people of color. That the city in which I worked was also one of the most infected places in the nation was, for a vaccine trial, a good thing, because it made it more likely that people would be exposed to the virus and made for a better test of vaccine efficacy. Could I help?

Of course I could and would help. People in Central Falls were infected, and too many had died. Only about 10 percent of the people in Central Falls could work from home, and the governor had allowed factories to stay open, so many people continued to work. They became infected at work and brought COVID-19 back into their densely packed houses. Whole families became infected. Many people lost their jobs or were laid off. The schools closed, putting our families under greater stress yet.

We then did something very unusual in the world of research. I proposed, and my colleague agreed, to fund the hiring of ten community residents, many of whom were out of work because of the pandemic, as health ambassadors. They'd walk the streets in bright orange hats and bright orange hoodies with yellow vests, face protectors, and N95 masks, encouraging people to mask up, distributing masks, and trying to enroll people in the vaccine trial. My colleague, as I stated above, agreed to fund this, and we found additional funding from another source and hired twenty-five community people, most of whom were doing health care work for the first time. Our health ambassadors were everywhere in Central Falls for a few months, patrolling the streets, handing out masks, attempting—not very successfully, I'm afraid—to enroll people in the vaccine trial, and counting the number of people who were masked. (We were 90 to 100 percent masked by our measure on most days, in the only place I know that measured and reported a masking percentage daily.) On cold or rainy days, the health ambassadors stood in stores and other public places, measuring temperatures and handing out masks. As soon as the vaccine became available, they worked to register people for it and they staffed our vaccination clinics. They encountered huge vaccine hesitancy and worked to counter that.

I can't prove that our health ambassadors blunted the intensity of the pandemic in Central Falls. We stayed the most infected place in the state, and one of the most infected places in the nation, mostly because our residents had to go out to work every day and came home to densely packed houses. But the amazing thing, from the perspective of the usual process of medical research, was that money from the research process flowed to a community at risk, a community of need, and was used to increase employment, resiliency, and connectedness as it was used to promote the research effort.

But that's not what medical research usually looks like.

Another story: About twenty-five years ago, an elderly patient I was caring for with early dementia told me that she was participating in a trial of a new Parkinson's drug, a trial organized by a physician and researcher I knew. The patient had gone to see the physician about her dementia. I knew that doctor only well enough to know that he had just left his longtime academic job to take a job in a private neurological practice that was for-profit and was engaged in for-profit research funded by pharmaceutical companies, a move too many physicians were making at that time, hoping to expand their incomes. I asked the patient, "What do you understand about the trial you are in?" She looked at me blankly. She had little or no understanding of the risks and benefits of that trial, as we might expect, because her dementia impacted her ability to understand and to make judgments about complex ideas. "Did they explain that you might be getting a placebo?" I asked. The poor lady looked at me like I was from Mars. "Did they explain that any new drug has risks, which differ for each drug—the risks of an allergic reaction, the risks of headaches or nausea or vomiting or skin rashes, that kind of thing?" The poor lady looked at me blankly. "Did they ask you to sign a paper giving your permission to be in the trial?" She had no understanding about that either.

We never talked about whether or not she was being paid for her time or transportation. The poor lady understood only that she was getting a powerful new medicine that was supposed to cure her Parkinson's disease. "Wait a second," I said. "I didn't know you *had* Parkinson's disease." I opened her chart, and sure enough there was nothing in her chart confirming that diagnosis. I was her primary care doctor. I took care of her and her family. I saw her once every three months or so. And all this was new to me.

When I called over to the specialist's office to get more information about the patient's diagnosis and treatment and this trial, I couldn't get the big man on the phone, as was usual when I called him. I spent about half an hour getting switched from secretary to secretary, from nurse to nurse, until I reached a resident or a fellow, the most junior physician who might be able to prescribe a new medicine. This was the guy who had enrolled the poor lady in this trial.

"Help me understand how you got this poor lady to give you informed consent," I said.

"She signed the paper," he said. "I have the paper right here."
"No, that's not the point," I said. "I'm not convinced she
even *has* Parkinson's disease. And I *know* she didn't give you
informed consent, because she's not capable of consent. You
guys are supposed to be neurologists. You are blinking trained
to access brain function and to recognize dementia and delir-
ium when it's present." ("Blinking" was probably not the word
I wanted to use, but I'm a polite guy even when riled.)

In retrospect, I did get impolite. And I demanded the
junior neurologist withdraw her from the trial, at least until
the diagnosis was confirmed by a senior neurologist and until
someone who had guardianship and was legally competent to
make decisions for the patient had given consent that was actually informed.

Of course, an hour later I got an angry call from the senior
neurologist. He accused me of interfering in critical research.
We had words. Two weeks later, he rejected a paper I'd written,
acting for a journal of which he was the editor. It was a very
good paper. Maybe an important paper. And I still have the
letter he wrote me, which gave grounds for rejecting the paper
that had nothing whatsoever to do with what was written in
the paper, because the rejection was really a rejection of my
position that it was not ethical for people who are patients to be
exploited for medical research, regardless of how important that
research appeared to be from the perspective of the researcher.
A couple of months later, I quit practicing medicine in disgust,
in part because this interaction proved to me that medicine as
a profession had become irretrievably corrupt.

Medical research is composed of the following: foundational
research to uncover the biological mechanism of disease, which
usually occurs in the laboratories of universities and is funded
by grants from the National Institutes of Health; drug discovery, or the biochemical, virological, and immunological search
for likely active compounds or substances that might be used
to treat disease, which occurs both in university laboratories

and in the laboratories of pharmaceutical companies or in a contracted laboratory; animal subject testing, which, again, usually occurs in a pharmaceutical company's laboratories or in contracted laboratories, but some occurs in university laboratories as well; and human subjects research, where compounds identified as likely to be safe and effective are tested on human beings. In addition, there is a fair amount of research that takes place in the process of development of new devices and new products used in health care that aren't drugs, as well as new processes that aren't either devices or drugs, for example: new artificial joints or heart valves, new monitoring devices or new kinds of defibrillators, and new techniques for helping people to change behaviors. All of this needs to be developed, tested, and proven safe. Testing new drugs, devices, and processes on human subjects occurs at pharmaceutical companies, at contracted university and hospital settings, and at contracted for-profit "medical research centers," which advertise for volunteer participants and pay them a small fee for their time. Human subjects research is overseen by institutional review boards (IRBs), organizations usually supported by universities and hospitals (originally) and now also by medical research companies and pharmaceutical companies, as was discussed in chapter 3. Now, as I described earlier, there are independent institutional review boards that run as for-profit businesses— so companies and entrepreneurs make money in the review process as well as in the process of conducting the research on human subjects itself, because there is just so much money to be made by developing and selling new medications, devices, and processes.

(There is so much money in health care that there are even big companies whose products are computer algorithms to help decide when an implantable defibrillator *isn't* needed or to show when a hospital or other health care provider is overtreating its patients. These are companies that make millions of dollars by researching and developing products to prevent the flagrant waste of money on products that the rest of the medical business enterprise works day and night to design—evidence of how out of control the medical-industrial complex has become and how good it is at extracting the resources of individuals and communities.)

The flip side of the research enterprise is a cost-benefit analysis that looks at the places all this money—the employment and the profits—ends up. How much are researchers paid for their time and their work? Where do people who have the high-paying jobs live? Who wins and who loses in the research enterprise?

Not surprisingly, scientists live in cities, though there isn't data that tells us in what part of those cities they live. Beijing, New York, Boston and Cambridge, San Francisco, Baltimore and Washington, Tokyo, Shanghai, Paris, Los Angeles, and Chicago had the most scientists as a portion of their populations in 2017.[1] Scientists as a group made an average salary of $70,238 per year in 2019, about 16 percent above the average American salary, with those in Boston and New York making substantially more, about $82,000 per year, with scientists in biotech making considerably more yet, $101,000 to $138,000.[2] Of course, there are thousands of other workers in the biotech research enterprise—lab techs, data analysts, computer programmers, and so forth, some of whom make the average annual wage of American workers or below. And there are plenty of people in the biotech enterprise who make lots more—doctors, venture capitalists, corporate lawyers, and investment bankers, for example, who make many times more than the average annual wage. But all these people live and work where scientists live and work: in our cities. As a standalone enterprise, the research process brings resources to cities and not to rural areas or even, directly, to suburbs.

Not surprisingly in the United States of 2021, most scientists are white men. In 2015, 49 percent of scientists and engineers were white men, 18 percent were white women, 14 percent were Asian men, 7 percent were Asian women, 3 percent were Black men, 2 percent were Black women, 4 percent were Latino men, and 2 percent were Latina women.[3] The disparities are striking.

Underneath and surrounding these disparities remains the question of colonialism. The profit generated from all this activity in communities of color is likely proportionately greater than the portion of the population they represent, because of the health effects of institutional racism on people of color, who carry a greater burden of illness and generate proportionately greater health care costs. This profit is likely proportionately greater in communities of color even despite the fact that people of color in the United States have less access to health care and despite the fact that health care costs consume a far greater proportion of the annual family income of households of color.[4]

Remember that the employment of people from those communities in the research enterprise has always been and remains far less than that of people from other communities.

What about the communities that supply research subjects? The role of diverse communities supplying research subjects cuts several different ways. On one hand, we want people from diverse communities to be research subjects so that new drugs and devices are tested on people with the same diversity of genetic composition and who have the same incidence and prevalence of disease as the people for whom the drugs and devices will be prescribed, so that we know the likely impact and safety profiles of those products. On the other hand, we want to make sure that people who are research subjects are fairly paid for their time, and we want to make sure that research subjects give true informed consent, that they really understand what they are being asked to do, and that they really understand the risks and potential benefits of their choice to be research subjects. This is particularly important because in most research, 50 percent of people participating will get a placebo, so that scientists can compare the active drug or device and its impact on the treated population with a matched population that isn't treated but that lives in the same place and is subject to the same environment.

It is critically important that research subjects, particularly those from poor or working backgrounds and those with life-threatening conditions, not be pushed into becoming subjects by ardent investigators who have something to gain from the research, in terms of publications and career advancement—ardent investigators who might be tempted to use unrealistic hopes, money, or just the social power imbalance that exists between themselves and people from poor and working communities. Finally, we want to make sure that if a study is well funded and well thought out, if payment for time is fair and realistic, and if there is no pressure on the part of researchers, people from poor and working communities have equal opportunity to participate if they so choose.

What does the data tell us about research subjects?

Actually, nothing. There is no compilation of demographic information about research subjects in the United States, or even around the world. We have no organized systemic understanding of whether research subjects are rich or poor, male or female, LGBTQ or straight, Black or white, English speaking or Spanish speaking, or speakers of another language. We don't know what parts of the country they come from, how old they are, how well or poorly they are paid, or how much they really understand about the research they participated in. Each trial has that data, of course. But we have no system to help us understand how effective we are at recruiting research subjects from many communities, no system to make sure that all communities are fairly represented, no way to know if what passes for informed consent is truly informed, and no yardstick to measure the way people are paid for participating, because there is no standard: Should you be paid minimum wage? Or should you be paid what the doctors, nurses, and researchers are paid by the hour? All we have are those forms people signed for each trial, moldering in a real or virtual drawer somewhere.

That said, a number of studies have suggested that women and minorities are significantly underrepresented in clinical research.[5] And few clinical trials offer interpreters, so it is likely that speakers of English are heavily overrepresented.

None of this is a surprise, of course. The history of clinical research is besmirched by too many stories of researchers blatantly exploiting people of color for their own benefit, ignoring the needs and values of those communities, and seeking only bodies to be experimented on—or to create profit from. The best known is the infamous Tuskegee experiment, the "Tuskegee Study of Untreated Syphilis in the Negro Male," in which 399 Black men with syphilis were followed, untreated, for thirty years *after* effective treatment was discovered so that US Public Health Service researchers could study the natural history of this known, often-fatal disease. What is less well known is the impact of that study on the communities from which those men came, as they unknowingly infected other people, infections that were all preventable.[6] Also well known is the story of Henrietta Lacks, a Black woman who died of cervical cancer in 1951 at age 31, and of the cells from her cervix, which were "harvested" without her knowledge or consent and have become the source of a cell line used by researchers all over the world, also without her knowledge or the knowledge and consent of her family.[7] These stories and too many others like them are known in communities of color and, quietly, in the medical community itself. They represent the history of a sort of scientific colonialism, on the one hand, but they have also come to be a roadblock to communities of color seeking useful and needed medical care. People don't want to be exploited. They don't want to be experimented on without their consent. And they often can't tell who in the medical community, which is now overwhelmingly for-profit, can be trusted not to exploit or to take advantage. So people in those communities sometimes avoid needed and useful medical care altogether or postpone needed treatment because of those fears.

What I've described so far is just the research activity in the US. The research activity of corporate entities that are based in the US and in other developed nations and that use subjects in developing nations around the world is also problematic, from the perspective of wealth extraction and colonialism.

Another story: I worked in Kenya for a month in 2005, in a tiny hospital in the western part of the country near the border of Uganda, a place beset by infectious disease—by malaria, tuberculosis, rabies, meningitis, and HIV. This place made me appreciate modern medicine in a new way, because in Kenya, medicine, with access to modern tools, actually saves lives, although many lives are still lost because there isn't enough medicine and there aren't enough health care workers. In Kenya, I heard stories about HIV research being conducted at a university about seventy-five miles away. The research there was generally thought of as ethical. People with HIV were treated and followed for years, and they even received a stipend for participating in the research, so the major clinical challenge was keeping in touch with the enrolled subjects and making sure they took their medicines every day, which is critical for HIV medicines to work.

But there was a hitch. People without HIV, people who lived in desperate poverty, sometimes tried to get infected with HIV. Once infected they celebrated, because once infected they could get on a trial and get a stipend, which provided them with an income they could never hope to earn themselves by working. It was better for poor Kenyans and their families for one of them to contract a potentially fatal disease than it was to live in dire poverty.

The HIV story is not about exploitation or colonialism per se. But it does illustrate the enormous ethical risks we take when we bring the medical-industrial enterprise of developed nations to the populations of developing nations, where the disparities in wealth are so great as to undermine the hope of any ethical transaction, however well intentioned.

It turns out that most clinical trials for drugs submitted for approval to the FDA have conducted at least part of their testing in other nations. Eighty-six percent of the first twenty-nine drugs submitted to the FDA for new drug approvals in 2017, for example, had been tested elsewhere.[8] It isn't possible to know how fairly those research subjects were paid, or much about the ethical standards that guided the trials, given that, as observed above, most clinical trials conducted by Big Pharma are now submitted to for-profit institutional review boards, which lack meaningful public accountability. In addition, many of the nations that host our clinical research are slow to get the drugs we test or develop there. A recent study showed that only 15 percent of thirty-four new drugs were approved in all countries where they were tested. Among the seventy countries that hosted research participants, 7 percent (five countries) got access to the drugs they helped test within one year of US approval, and 31 percent (twenty-two countries) did so within five years. This means 62 percent of those countries still did not have such access five years after they hosted the research. Not surprisingly, African nations got access to those drugs last.[9]

Only about a quarter of all drug sales around the world are to other nations—about $100 billion of the $375 billion of US drug makers' sales come from overseas.[10] So all this international research activity supports domestic profits. We are mining, if you will, the biological experience of people in other nations for information about *our* drugs, which are then submitted to the regulatory agency of *our* government for evaluation and are intended for use in the United States—although there is still plenty of money to be made by selling those drugs in developing nations, as I'll discuss later. No gunships in sight for this one. Only financial advantage taken of other people's economic misfortunes, which compel them to volunteer for drug trials that will benefit Americans first. We might as well be asking people in other nations to sell their plasma, or their sperm, or their ova, to create children elsewhere for us to raise here—all of which actually happens. Health care for people? Or for profit? Whose profit? And whose loss?

People in other nations *do* benefit from medical research done in those places by US pharmaceutical companies and device manufacturers. When a new treatment is discovered, the public health benefits of that discovery flow to the populations of other nations as well as to US citizens and residents—and that happens, at least sometimes. But the bulk of US pharma research is devoted to medications that have sales potential in the US market, not to medications and vaccines that have huge public health impact. Polio vaccination has had a big international public health impact, and we are achingly close to eradicating polio from the planet. But the foundational research on polio vaccine in the 1950s was carried out by an international collaboration led by Jonas Salk that was not-for-profit. The treatment for infant diarrhea, a major killer of infants around the world, is simple rehydration solution, which can't even be patented. Research into malaria and schistosomiasis and even river blindness is funded mostly by nonprofits—many of which are funded in turn by US billionaires, some of whom made some of their money from health care in the US, an interesting ethical paradox if ever there was one. HIV and COVID-19 research were mostly for-profit. It took a major international effort to get US and European pharmaceutical companies to make HIV medications that had been tested in developing nations available to the people who lived in those nations.

And there has been similar arm wrestling around making the COVID-19 vaccine available to developing nations, regardless of where those vaccines were tested. As I write this, in August 2021, between 50 and 90 percent of people in developed nations have been vaccinated against COVID-19, but only 31 percent of people in the developing world have been vaccinated. Among the world's poorest nations, it's 1 percent.[11]

Even so, there are endless trade disputes around the patent rights of US pharmaceutical companies in developing nations, disputes that have threatened to torpedo several international and trade agreements, as US pharmaceutical companies always want to see that their patent rights are protected, even at the expense of international public health.

So even when there is downstream benefit from pharmaceutical research to the people in developing nations, that benefit is an *unintended consequence* of the research. Big Pharma research in other nations is for us, not for those nations and their people. Some people in colonies did benefit from the process of colonialization: some got educated, and some learned business or trades. But as with true colonialism, it is the dominant nation that benefits most from the colonial interaction and the dominant people who profit, while the colonized people are left to make do the best they can with what that dominant nation discards. Research exists to enrich the researchers. Pharma and other research leave the research subjects, their nations, and their cultures to fend for themselves.

CHAPTER NINE

Medical Colonialism as, Well, Colonialism Itself

S o far, I've focused on what might be called virtual colonialism: the ways in which the state is a party to wealth that is extracted from communities under the banner of health care. Most of that discussion has been about domestic "colonialism," about how crony capitalists get their hands on the levers of the state and use it to drain communities in the US of their resources. But what about how the United States as a nation uses its market and military power to rob other nations of their resources under the banner of health care? What about the good old-fashioned gunboat-diplomacy kind of colonialism itself?

The United States uses our military and economic power abroad to generate profit in many ways: using drugs and vaccines, using research, using health professions, and using a number of other products that have adverse health effects, products that we dump on other nations. Those products make people sick. And then we show up, grinning from ear to ear, and offer to sell them medications and devices to fix the health problems our products caused in the first place.

I will never forget the well-intentioned work of a friend and trusted colleague, an endocrinologist who had spent his life helping people in the US control their diabetes, who convinced the members of a hospital medical staff to donate $10,000 for a machine that tests for hemoglobin A1c, which can be used to diagnose diabetes and assess its control and which had just come into wide use in the US, to a medical school and hospital in rural Kenya. That machine, which used expensive reagents and required a reliable supply of electricity, was of uncertain value in a place where the major public health threats were malaria, infant dehydration, tuberculosis, HIV, meningitis, typhoid, and rabies, most of which can be prevented by simple public health measures like providing clean water and bed nets, clearing swamps, immunizing dogs and cats against rabies, and making sure people have safe and healthy housing.

That hemoglobin A1c machine was most probably never going to be used, given the cost of its reagents, but if it had been used, it was more likely to cause more problems than it solved. The control of diabetes meant the use of drugs or insulin, for most people, and the supply of those drugs was intermittent in rural Kenya. What did the diagnosis and treatment of diabetes mean for the people who had the test, if it showed diabetes after all? Some of those people were likely to just give up when they confronted the difficulty of treatment. But some were likely to spend all their available money on these drugs, and much of the available money of their families and villages, trying to treat a disease that was extremely difficult to treat in that setting. We know the health impact of treating diabetes in the US, where we have a different infrastructure and have had almost a hundred years to study diabetes in our environment, where infectious diseases have long been controlled but where our diet is too calorie rich, where most people don't get enough exercise as part of their daily life, where cigarette smoking was once endemic but is now less prevalent, and where high-tech medical treatment for things like kidney failure, often caused by diabetes, is available everywhere.

The impacts on population health of treating diabetes in the developing world are unstudied and unknown, and because of the many other and more serious risks that exist in Kenya, I can't tell you anything about the most likely outcome, about whether or not we would be likely to extend the treated person's life or reduce the likelihood of disability from one of the known complications of diabetes—heart disease, stroke, and kidney failure—because of the multitude of those other risks and the

way they dwarf the meaning of effective treatment of diabetes from a public health perspective. But I can tell you with
certainty that anyone in rural Kenya who is treated for diabetes
is likely to spend lots of money for drugs and supplies and that
most of that money is likely to end up in the pockets of owners of
corporate shares in the US, Canada, and Western Europe. That
money might well be better spent on the school fees of children
in the community of the person with diabetes, or on bed nets
or clean water.

Of course, my well-intentioned and very ethical colleague
didn't mean for that kind of wealth transfer to occur. But that's
exactly the problem. No one means for Western medicine to
create wealth extraction. No one means for Western medicine
to impoverish poor communities in developing nations. But
the spread of Western medicine into poor communities often
causes that impoverishment anyway, exactly because of how
it is structured: expensive products, made far away, controlled
by patents owned in other nations, instead of local treatments
delivered by local people that help maintain local wealth in
communities that control their own destinies.

The transfer of wealth under the guise of health care is happen-
ing around the world in a big way, so it is worth understanding
where and how that transfer occurs. US pharma generates about
$300 billion in sales of drugs and vaccines to developing nations.
"Emerging markets have now overtaken the EU5 economies
(Germany, France, Italy, the UK, and Spain) in pharmaceutical spending," according to an article published by McKinsey
and Company, a US consulting firm, "with a total market size
of USD 281 billion compared with the EU5's USD 196 billion in
2014."[1] The "opportunity" for US pharmaceutical companies
results from the presence of infectious diseases, which can be
prevented by vaccines and treated with antibiotics, but it also
results from a shift in the burden of disease to chronic diseases,
which require long-term medications. As incomes rise in these
developing nations, as people get access to a more reliable food

supply, as people move to cities, and as the average life expectancy grows, people in these nations now *do* develop obesity, hypertension, diabetes, heart disease, and cancer, diseases that demand long-term treatment, so perhaps my well-intentioned colleague was prescient when he had us buy that A1c machine thirty years ago.

"Lucky us!" pharma must be saying to itself. "The export of fast food and urbanized lifestyles has created many more potential customers for us!" Remember the triangle of our original colonialism? Our ships brought sugarcane from the West Indies, processed that sugarcane into rum, took the rum to Africa and sold it there, bought human beings as slaves, and transported those human beings to the West Indies and the US to be sold as slaves. The proceeds from those sales then allowed that cycle to begin again.

Now we have a new cycle: Urbanize developing nations. Send them fast food and enough medicine to extend their life spans. Watch them develop chronic disease. Sell them medicine to treat the chronic disease. Then let the cost of medicine impoverish them, which keeps them stressed, so they develop more chronic disease, which allows the sale of more medicine, and so the cycle continues, generating significant profits in the process.

The products are different. The processes are different. But the dynamics remain the same: richer nations profit from the misfortune of poorer places, help create misfortune in those places, and spread that misfortune as the cycle repeats itself.

Pharma now uses a complex approach to the marketing of its products to developing nations, which is called an "access-driven commercial model" by McKinsey and Company, which created it. McKinsey recommends that pharmaceutical companies use an eight-point strategy to make sure people in developing nations with chronic disease have access to medical care so that they can be diagnosed with those diseases, and it then recommends that pharmaceutical companies "work with" government purchasers and regulators to make sure their

drugs are correctly priced for the markets of focus and then
follow through to make sure those products are then purchased:
"Best-in-class organizations develop the skills to do so and hire
senior government affairs managers who can provide appropriate support to policy makers."[2] Which perhaps is a nice way of
saying, "Use lobbying and maybe a little bribery when necessary
to get these products sold."

Some pharmaceutical sales to developing nations accrue to
US pharma companies because of the power of their research
and development, which finds new drugs and develops new
vaccines early, research and development that is often hard
to copy quickly. So some of the value of pharma comes from
its intellectual property, which is always patent protected. But
some of the income comes from identifying and developing
new markets, creating access, and marketing itself. "Pharma
emerging markets carry high hopes for investors," wrote Maya
Tannoury and Zouhair Attieh in *Current Therapeutic Research*.
"With patent expiration, changes in disease patterns and the
increasing sale of generics and biosimilars, pharma industry
profits from these markets can be astronomical."[3]

Even so, those new markets would not be profitable without patent protection. And patent protection would not exist
without the World Trade Organization (WTO), which corralled
all nations into the enforcement of pharmaceutical company
patents, using international trade to put pressure on nations
to respect those patents.

The World Trade Organization has a critical role in the wealth
extraction process. The WTO came into being in 1995 and exists
to promote global trade, using a process of consensus to keep
the global-trade playing field level. Only fourteen nations are
not members of the WTO. All members, which means all other
countries, are bound by WTO agreements. The WTO agree-
ment on Trade Related Aspects of Intellectual Property Rights
included patent protection for pharmaceuticals, so that by
1995, almost all nations had agreed to protect the patents of

pharmaceutical companies, which usually last at least twenty years.

There are some exemptions, such as allowing local manufacturing in the setting of public health emergencies, but those exemptions are rarely used—and are usually challenged by pharmaceutical companies when invoked, arguing that patent protection is necessary for them to engage in research and development because only patent protection allows the recovery of their substantial investment in research. Even so, nothing in the WTO's process creates an obligation on the part of pharma to share intellectual property or even license that intellectual property to developing nations when there is a public health emergency in the developing world. The logic of the marketplace suggests that such licensure, which was sought by many countries for the COVID-19 vaccines but refused by pharma, is dangerous to the profit potential of pharma companies. Once licensed, generic drug companies can learn the processes by which drugs and vaccines are created. That knowledge would likely allow them to produce similar drugs of their own and compete with the more established companies for future products. From the perspective of intellectual property, once you let the genie out of the bottle, there's no getting it back in. Note that many of these drugs and vaccines were developed by researchers from developing nations who moved to the US or other developed nations to work for pharma (see the comments on research and the health professional workforce later in this chapter) and that many people who live in developing nations participate not only in the clinical trials of the drugs and vaccines that work, but also in the trials of the many drugs and vaccines that are never brought to market but are an essential part of the research effort to produce products that are safe and effective. So the people in developing nations participate, in more ways than one, in the development of these important drugs and vaccines—but then the countries from which these people come are asked to pay through the nose for access to the sometimes lifesaving results of their own contributions.

Here's the gunboat: if a developing nation wants to be able to engage in international trade in any meaningful way, it must join the WTO and swallow pharma's claim about patents. Once a developing nation accepts the WTO's intellectual property rules, that nation's ability to protect its own resources disappears.

The world has changed. While there are plenty of developed nations with strong militaries and strong economies, the need for an actual gunboat has vanished. Now developing nations are held hostage by their own desire for trade and development, which they can't get without belonging to the WTO. This international system, which favors international trade over local development, enforces the ability of pharma companies and others to transfer resources from poor places to richer ones and from public entities, like the governments of those developing nations, to private pockets, if those governments want to protect the health and safety of their own people.

Economists argue about the long-term net effects of globalization and international trade. Certainly, there are far fewer people living in dire poverty, as a percentage of the world's population, than there were a hundred years ago (although the *number* of people living in dire poverty has likely remained the same or even increased as the world's population has increased). Certainly, the centralization of wealth and the disparities between rich and poor have also grown. There isn't a good measure to answer the question "Are we better off or not since globalization?" since globalization itself may be just an inevitable consequence of developing technologies. But the coincidental challenges to democracy, urbanization, and climate change that all these forces have produced raise worrisome questions about how globalization impacts the human project at the end of the day.

That said, one wonders just how pharma managed to seek and win patent protection for its medications through the WTO process. Could it be that the culture of technology is inherently biased? That the processes and ideology of a culture that creates profit out of labor-saving devices, speed, and so-called efficiency always favor those with power and capital? That Big Pharma had the capital and influence needed to sway a process that inherently favors the acquisition of capital and influence? That Big Pharma had enough money to sway the WTO process into accepting the argument that patent protection was needed to advance public health when there was little evidence for that claim and plenty of reason for thinking that claim isn't true?

Much of our culture and many of our organizations are like beaters in an old-style quail hunt, driving the birds toward hunters who are waiting, shotguns loaded, behind a blind. "Access management" marketing, disease creation, international "aid," and the World Bank drive other nations toward that blind, otherwise known as the World Trade Organization and its intellectual property rules. Then the WTO "fires its guns" on those nations, which we bring home and carve up to eat for dinner.

We don't live in a world where nations are free agents anymore. In our world, it isn't nations that have the most power to leverage, and power isn't always military power. Now organizations like the World Bank and the World Trade Organization can make most nations do their bidding, although a few meganations—the US, China, the EU, Russia, India, and Brazil—can and do have significant military and financial impact on the well-being and wealth of their neighbors. Today, multinational corporations leverage the power of those global institutions and meganations as they extract resources from countries around the world.

And wealth extraction doesn't occur only between nations. It also occurs within nations. So global corporations, leveraging the power of worldwide institutions and the meganations, have become adept at extracting wealth from market segments and local communities all over the globe, even inside the meganations. As a result, working people, people of color, and even people who used to think of themselves as middle class in the

US have seen their wealth shrink and their agency diminish over the last fifty years, just as people in rural China were left behind in the Chinese economic expansion, along with people in rural areas in Ireland and Italy. At the same time, people in Bangladesh, India, and much of Africa have seen their standard of living rise a little, but their communities have also weakened as their young people move into cities, and their agency—their ability to act individually and in concert with others in a way that is meaningful to their lives—has vanished.

Small but meaningful improvements in the standard of living are used as the social justification for urbanization and the rise of technological society. People are encouraged to think of those improvements in standard of living as a substitute for wealth. But isn't wealth really the richness of life in a community? Doesn't human life develop meaning when people live together in concert with nature? When family and social interactions are rich and varied? And when there is time to see one another, be together, watch the sun set, the moon rise, and feel warm or cool breezes blowing in from the mountains or the sea?

Thus, it is time for us to understand colonialism not just as the wealth extraction that occurs when the gunboat of a wealthy place sails into the harbor of a poorer place and demands tribute, but as any activity that leverages power relationships (military, financial, sexual, or intellectual) to strip individuals and their communities of their agency in order to create profit (material, military, intellectual, or sexual) for others.

This analysis of pharma's ability to use the WTO process to protect its ability to extract profits from developing nations suggests that colonialism itself has become globalized and transnational. Once, you needed a gunboat. Now all you need are lawyers and lobbyists—and you no longer need either gunboats or countries. Colonialism leverages state power writ large, the state power of a global commercial and political enterprise, the state power of a new class of capitalists—the capitalists who exploit our collective willingness to be led, to abandon our agency as individuals and communities and exchange that agency for a few cheap products, cheap ideas, images flashing across a screen, or the often-illusory promise of protection from disease or even death itself. This new megacolonialism, built on the lust for simple satisfactions that exists in all of us, leveraged to become money and power, too often eclipses our also human need for relationship and community, in terms of how populations of people can be mobilized to act or not act, and for what.

But the process of megacolonialism is inherently threatening to the existence of democracy and community. Now decisions are made in distant places by unelected elites, following the logic of the marketplace, which is the logic of speed, scalability, power, and profit, not the logic of place, patience, and community. What is not clear is whether we can turn the arc of history away from speed, scalability, power, profit, and social control; turn it back toward community, democracy, and human-scaled development; and recover meaning in the human project once again.

Like pharmaceuticals, other products that are medically related are sold to nations around the world. The story of infant formula is the best known. Beginning in the 1960s and '70s, Nestlé and other companies marketed infant formula to developing nations. Those companies argued that their formulas were somehow better than human milk, and in the process they discouraged millions of women from breastfeeding. For most children, of course, the opposite is true: human milk transmits antibodies that prevent disease, while formula requires a source of clean water that is sometimes unavailable in developing nations. Human milk is free, while formula removes disposable income. And breastfeeding helps create a bond between mother and child that is indelible, while anyone can formula-feed a baby without establishing any meaningful human relationship. The marketing of formula leverages mothers' desires to be sure that their children are adequately fed, as well as a certain shyness and societal stigma about breastfeeding in public, and some ideas about ease, convenience, and modernity, although many of those ideas are created by marketers just to sell formula itself.

But breast is best. That is the unanimous consensus of the medical and public health communities. After a huge international outcry in the mid-1970s about how Nestlé used free samples, used the media in developing nations to make breastfeeding sound difficult, time consuming, embarrassing, primitive, and even dangerous, and made hospitals their agents,[4] the company and others changed many of their marketing practices, after WHO (!) banned the promotion of infant formula as being in any way comparable to human breast milk, in 1981.[5]

Yet both the sales and the marketing of infant formula in developing nations continues. According to Professor George Kent of the University of Hawaii, writing in the *International Breastfeeding Journal*, "In the Middle East and North Africa, the baby food market has been growing at a compound annual growth rate of 11.2 per cent during 2007–2012. US$41 billion was spent on milk formula globally in 2013. Retail sales of infant formula in China alone are expected to reach US$27 billion by 2017."[6]

And it is not just drugs and infant formula. The marketing of tobacco to low- and middle-income countries exploded once tobacco-control efforts started reducing tobacco use in developed nations, so that by 2030, 80 percent of tobacco-related deaths will occur in those developing nations.[7] While the medical-industrial complex doesn't sell tobacco products itself, it will be the beneficiary of the demand that tobacco-related illness creates for medication and devices in the developing world. US and European pharma doesn't sell tobacco either. But pharma does make products—drugs and nicotine-replacement gums and patches—that help treat tobacco addiction, and Big Pharma strongly supports US and European trade policy to protect its patents in developing nations, policy that also protects the interests of tobacco companies and industrial food producers as they spread their products around the world, creating the illnesses that their brother and sister companies profit from treating.

Medical tourism leverages the lower cost of medical and dental procedures in other nations. Insurance companies and employers pay for people to travel the world, seeking bargain heart-valve replacements, knee replacements, hip replacements, plastic surgery, dental implants, or in vitro fertilization at discounts of 50 to 90 percent off US prices. Sometimes people who are uninsured or underinsured travel themselves, looking for bargains. The actual number of people who do so and the actual amount of money that changes hands is unknown, but it has been estimated to be in the range of $5 to $10 billion a year.[8]

On the face of it, medical tourism is the opposite of colonialism. Resources flow to developing nations, not from developing nations.

But think about it again. The hospitals that are used in other countries are paid for by the people of those countries. The health professionals who do the surgery, the recovery, and the follow-up care are trained by those nations for their own people. Americans are thus "harvesting" the investments of others for their own use and "extracting" the ore of health care. While the hospitals and health professionals are paid for their services, and likely fairly paid from their perspectives, no one measures the opportunity cost of the lost value of services that might have been provided to citizens of the nations where the care happens. Sounds like wealth extraction to me.

But perhaps the most damaging kind of real colonialism is the harvesting of the developing world's health professional workforce. In 2015, there were 209,367 physicians, or 24 percent of all physicians practicing in the United States, who had graduated from foreign medical schools. Of those physicians, 58 percent were not American citizens. In that same year, 29,654 resident physicians were graduates of foreign medical schools, or 25 percent of all resident physicians in the US—58 percent of whom were not American citizens. That means there were 121,432 practicing physicians and 17,199 resident physicians working here, people who had come from India, Pakistan, Canada, Egypt, and Iran but also from Kenya, Liberia, Nigeria, Guatemala, the Dominican Republic, Haiti, Croatia, Syria, Jordan, Israel, Bangladesh, and many other countries, particularly those in the developing world. They practice all specialties but make up more than 25 percent of all internists, family physicians, psychiatrists, pathologists, and neurologists—the lower-paid and less "competitive" US specialties (with the exception of pediatrics, one of our lowest-paid specialties, which is about 20 percent international medical graduates).[9] About 8 percent of US registered nurses, which is about 219,000 in all, are estimated to be foreign educated, and 80 percent are from developing or lower-income countries like the Philippines, Jamaica, Guatemala, El Salvador, Honduras, Nigeria, Liberia, India, Pakistan, Bangladesh, and the countries of the Russian Federation.[10]

From the perspective of US hospitals and US community health centers, foreign workforce is a great thing. It ensures there is enough workforce to meet the needs of US residents. From the perspective of the health professionals who come here, the US need for workforce is fantastic. It provides a pathway to enter the US, still regarded around the world as a nation of freedom and opportunity—and many foreign professionals who enter on J-1 visas or through other special programs are allowed to stay and become US citizens, and taxpaying citizens at that.

But from the perspective of developing nations, the entry of foreign-trained health professionals into the US is a disaster. These professionals are trained at the expense of their home nations. They are trained on the bodies of their fellow citizens, learning from doing, and by using the cadavers of their fellow citizens to learn anatomy. Many developing nations have a single medical and nursing school and produce few health professional graduates every year, so that every health professional is desperately needed to care for thousands of people in places where there are no doctors and nurses. But it is hard for a poor country to compete with the US, where salaries are many times greater, where we have freedom of speech and a high standard of living. The few countries that pay health professionals many times the average income still usually don't come close to paying what health professionals earn in the US.

Liberia, for example, one of the poorest nations on earth, has a single medical school that produces just thirteen physicians a year—and needs hundreds, particularly after the Ebola epidemic of 2014–2015, which killed about 30 percent of its health professionals. But most of its physicians and many of its nurses emigrate. It has a well-thought-out system of community health centers—but very few well-trained health professionals to staff them. As a result, Liberia has one of the highest infant mortality rates in the world and among the world's shortest life expectancies, even as most of its physicians and nurses emigrate to the US and Western Europe as soon as they can.

So our gain is the loss of those developing nations, whose need is often much greater than ours.

How can the impact of medical colonialism on the developing world be addressed? First, the World Trade Organization and the World Bank need to change. These important international organizations need to review the data and change policy based on what the data really show, which is that pharmaceutical research and development rarely impacts the public's health, and so there is no reason to protect pharmaceutical patents in developing nations. Once in a generation, there is the emergence of an infectious disease threat like Ebola or COVID-19, but the income earned by pharma in developed nations is more than enough to support its research and development of vaccines and treatments for those outbreaks. Indeed, the World Bank should consider directly funding research and development for vaccines and diseases that are global health threats and supporting the manufacture and distribution of those treatments so that they can be distributed to all the world's citizens for free.

Funding international research and development to prevent pandemics will help the world's people to stay healthy. Healthy people, and not patents, are the best pathway to robust markets and economic growth, though the humanitarian justification for funding this research and supply ought to be adequate for getting the World Bank and the WTO to act. We cannot and should not make world trade contingent on protecting the intellectual property of a few companies in a few nations if we expect to have a healthy world community of democracies and durable world peace. That intellectual property, so-called, is really the property of all people in all nations, who have contributed to the development of knowledge as a world community with a collective history. That intellectual property should never be said to be owned by anyone, despite the military, legal, and financial might that is currently brought to bear on that knowledge—and that intellectual property should never be allowed to be used by some of us to extract rent from the rest of us.

Then, the US should change how we do health professional training and recruitment, acting like the leader of the free world in health care instead of unjustly claiming that position. We should learn from Cuba, which, despite its many failures in the arena of human rights and democracy, understood how to use health care and medicine as humanitarian outreach and as the cornerstone of its foreign relations. The Cubans bring foreign students from developing nations around the world—even from US inner cities, many of which look like developing nations from the perspective of economics and public health—and train them to be doctors and nurses on the condition that they go back to their home countries and serve the poor.

"The Latin American School of Medicine, or ELAM (Escuela Latinoamericana de Medicina), was established by the Cuban government in 1999," according to Steve Dubb, writing in the *Nonprofit Quarterly* in 2018. "The school is designed to provide free medical education to students drawn from throughout the world. To date, an estimated 28,500 students from 103 countries have graduated from ELAM, of whom 170 are from the US; of the 4,690 students enrolled as of 2017, about 1.8 percent (83 students) are from the US."[11] Even more impressive, 50 percent of the ELAM graduates from the US are Black and Latino. In the US, about *6 percent* of all medical students are Black and Latino, in a nation that is about 32 percent Black and Latino. Who has it right?

I've often thought about the medical schools of Liberia and Cape Verde, for example. As I've mentioned, Rhode Island, where I live, has large Liberian and Cape Verdean populations. Brown University's Alpert Medical School has students and residents who treat, and thus learn on, these populations, but those students and residents have scant relationships with the medical schools of either country. (Brown has a similarly scant relationship with Rhode Island itself. Most physicians who practice in Rhode Island believe about only 10 percent of its medical students come from Rhode Island.[12]) What would it look like, I have often wondered, if faculty and students from Brown went to those countries to help support *their* medical schools and to give our medical students exposure to the cultures of both of those places, where infectious diseases and their complications are seen much more frequently than they are seen here. US medical students often go through their training without seeing a case of rabies, malaria, disseminated tuberculosis, or even measles. What would it be like to have students, residents, and faculty from those countries come here to study with us, shoulder to shoulder, with the expectation (and requirement) that they return to their own countries and bring their knowledge and expertise back with them?

Now imagine what the world and the US would look like if the US adopted a similar program to Cuba's. Imagine what the world and the US would look like if we went one step further, if we tripled or quadrupled the size of medical and nursing schools and brought in fifty thousand students a year from developing nations on the condition that they return to their native countries and practice there among the poor for at least ten years. These bigger medical and nursing schools would allow us to train all the health professionals we need for our own population, so we could then stop draining the world of critical public health resources that we use mostly to support the medical-industrial complex of the US. But it would also allow us to train thousands of young health professionals from around the world. Imagine what the world would look like if the US began *supporting* the medical and nursing schools of developing nations rather than draining them of their best trainees, instead sending them faculty and some students on rotation to learn with foreign colleagues. Imagine what medicine and health care around the world would be like if the medical and nursing schools we supported had more robust faculties and better resources.

If we helped start schools of pharmacy in those nations and taught them how to manufacture their own generic drugs . . .

What would happen? First, the health of the population of the world might improve, at least a little—with the health of children being impacted most, because, truth be told, health care and medicine don't impact the health of populations very much, outside of the effect of vaccination against infectious disease on the life expectancy of children and the infant mortality rate. The economic well-being of other nations might improve as well, because some of the money they are spending unnecessarily now on pharma and on technology might be spent on education, housing, and public safety (which might well improve the health of the population of adults!) once their health professionals understood the public health impacts of these choices. The image of the US might improve as well—and might move from one of a nation that talks about freedom and democracy, is rich beyond imagination, invades other countries from time to time, and then leaves them flat to fend for themselves when fashions in the US change, to one of a place that is the beacon of freedom, democracy, and hope after all, a place that other nations and other people would want to emulate, not just emigrate to.

At the same time, and perhaps perversely, all that activity would open huge opportunities for pharma and other kinds of enterprises, as people around the world would look even more enthusiastically for our know-how and our processes, so long as we kept those products and processes affordable. The power of the professional traction that would occur can't be overstated. It exists now, when the few physicians and other health professionals who were trained here and then go home to practice have a difficult case and call or email an old professor. And that professional traction also exists now because of our medical and nursing journals, which are read by health professionals all around the world. But imagine, in addition to all that, a world in which thousands of physicians and nurses in every nation in the developing world were trained here or taught by American professors of medicine, nursing, dentistry, physical therapy, and pharmacy. Those professors would then become the people to call or email whenever their former students had a perplexing case or a patient who needed a level of care not available locally.

The downside, of course, is that US pharma could lose a market worth $290 billion a year. But pharma could expand that market, if they approached it in an enlightened way, by leveraging all those professors and their students, on the one hand, and by bringing low-cost generics to the huge population of the developing world in a way that is affordable. We as a nation, of course, might then be accused of a new kind of medical imperialism, not just medical colonialism. But think of the pushback we might offer to such accusations! The US, spreading population health. The US, spreading health democracy and, through that health democracy, spreading democracy itself. The US, spreading life, liberty, and the pursuit of happiness. *USA! USA! USA!* Let's do it, and then just let them try to damn us with that faint praise!

CHAPTER TEN

COVID-19

I n the COVID-19 pandemic, the greatest public health failure in history, we saw the chickens of medical colonialism come home to roost. COVID-19 is a new coronavirus that evolved in animals and crossed over to human beings—or was created in a laboratory in Wuhan, China, and was either released or escaped, depending on whose story and whose disinformation campaign you want to fall prey to this week. Coronaviruses are cold viruses. They aren't really very dangerous. They tend to live in the nose and are easily passed from person to person, but they don't harm the body very much most of the time, compared to other viruses—Ebola, measles, and HIV—that really do a fair amount of harm. COVID-19 was a problem because it was new to human beings and few adults had robust immunity to it, so it was likely to infect the entire human population quickly, because we are now so densely populated and mobile, and it was likely to kill the old, the sick, the immunocompromised, and relatively few others unless we outsmarted it, controlled its spread, developed a vaccine, and got the world's population vaccinated in a short amount of time.

The good news is that we developed a vaccine quickly, something the medical-industrial complex is pretty good at. The bad news is that we totally failed, as a world community, to prevent the spread of this new virus. We failed to get the world community vaccinated rapidly enough to save all the lives that could have and should have been saved. Over 5.64 million deaths by January 2022, two years after its emergence. Over 850,000

American deaths. Some countries—New Zealand, Hong Kong,
Australia, Korea, Japan, perhaps China (no one believes their
numbers; they completely failed to prevent COVID-19 from
spreading to the rest of the world and refuse to own that fact,
but they probably do have relatively fewer infections and deaths
because of their authoritarian approach to public health), and
a few other places—successfully prevented widespread disease
by using well-thought-out population movement control and
strong personal and community discipline. But the US, most
of Europe, South and Central America, India, Africa, Indonesia,
and Russia all failed miserably at the kind of organization and
discipline necessary to prevent massive spreading of this virus
before their populations were immunized.

The vaccine was ready and approved in December 2020. But
the world community completely failed to scale up production
and vaccinate most people. By August 2021, only 31 percent of
the world's population, or about two billion people, had had one
dose of the vaccine, and only 1.7 percent of people in low-income
countries had been vaccinated at all. By February 2022, only 61
percent of the world's population had received a single dose
(which is not very protective against the Omicron variant) and
only 10 percent of people in low-income countries had received
that first dose, and these numbers count some two billion people
who got Sinovac, the Chinese vaccine that doesn't work well
at all.[1] That means that we can expect ten to twenty million
deaths or more, the bulk of which are still preventable, right
now, if we act as a world community trying to protect human
life instead of acting as if medicine is a business that aims to
maximize profit. The failure to immunize the world population
quickly means that the virus has had many chances to mutate,
and consequently many new variants have evolved, making the
virus even more difficult to control, even in the places that have
done well controlling it thus far.

The impact of medical colonialism on the pandemic can be
seen in how poorly the world responded in general, in how slow
we've been at getting vaccines to the world population, and in

how the US failed to vaccinate many of its own people quickly, a consequence of the way the processes of colonialism have, over fifty years, stripped communities of civic trust and of their ability to protect (and in this case, to vaccinate) themselves. We have lost our agency. We have stopped, as nations and as people, standing up together to halt this threat and to save human lives, to prevent millions of preventable deaths. We are waiting for others—for pharma, for consultants, for insurance companies and hospitals—to stop the virus. Medical colonialism has made us forget that we are the agents of our own future and made us forget that the colonialists exist only to sell us something and create profit for themselves.

The initial breakdown of response centered in China, Europe, and the US and was a consequence of the Chinese failure to act quickly to restrict population movement in and out of Wuhan in early January 2020 and of the failures in Europe and the US to do the same. An estimated 388,287 people flew from China to other nations in the world in January 2020, when COVID-19 was spreading widely in Wuhan.[2] Corrupt officials in Wuhan, responding to political pressures in a state that is not even close to a democracy, suppressed information about this emerging viral threat, in part so they could throw a very big party for forty thousand people in late January 2020, a party that was meant to prop up their political support. During that period of that failure to act, many people also traveled from Wuhan to other places in China and around the world. The US, which too often puts commerce as its first consideration, failed to restrict travel to the US from China until the end of January 2020; Europe also failed to act.

The context was and is a world in which travel is a critical feature of a global economy that is focused on profit. Travel is big business and is a big business tool, as companies send employees around the world to cut deals, develop products, and spread sales strategies. (Indeed, at least two early major superspreader events—the Biogen meeting in Boston and the Webasto meeting in Stockdorf, Germany—were corporate meetings that involved people from China. In the Webasto meeting, attended by a Chinese employee from Wuhan, at least sixteen people were infected on January 23, 2020. And then they or their contacts went skiing in Ischgl, Austria, and brought the virus to a ski resort, and then the virus spread from the ski resort to Italy, Iceland, Great Britain, and a number of other places.) In this way, the *infection* was caused by a virus, perhaps, but the *pandemic* resulted from the culture of global commerce, which exists for wealth extraction and uses the tools of colonialism to extract wealth. So the flip side of wealth extraction and colonialism is the pandemic spread of a virus that isn't terribly dangerous and can be well managed, as long as the public health infrastructure of nations is intact and the value of human life is thought more important than the value of commerce itself.

The failure to vaccinate the world's population quickly is an immediate consequence of medical colonialism. If we believed that human life was holy and that the preservation of human life was our primary objective, we would have set aside all other work by July 2020 (when vaccines went into clinical trials), scaled up the worldwide vaccine production capacity, and then, in December 2020, devoted all available workforce to the vaccination effort. But the underlying ideology—that profit is at the center of human affairs—held sway. Even so, we used state power, in the form of financial support to the tune of $10.5 billion, to develop the vaccines. In other nations, governments distributed the vaccines and by doing so became unwitting agents of the pharmaceutical companies that created and marketed the vaccines, creating profit but also a public good, which was vaccination of the population itself.

In the United States, we allowed private corporate enterprises to manufacture and distribute the vaccines, usually to state and local government but also to other private enterprises like CVS and Walgreens. Because of this, the effort itself has to be seen as private enterprises creating private profit out of public funding, using government as their agent in the distribution of the vaccine, with a public good as one intended outcome (for government) but with private profit as the driver for the private enterprises that were engaged in this activity. Interestingly and as described in chapter 5, in the US, physicians and nurse-prac-titioners practicing primary care, the traditional vaccinators of the public, as well as the emergency management agencies of city and town governments, were usually excluded from the vaccination process. In the US, most vaccination was carried out at mass vaccination clinics run by state departments of health using Washington-based contractors like Alvarez & Marsal or John Snow, Inc., or occurred at chain retail pharmacies like CVS and Walgreens.[3] (About a third of all vaccines in the US, or 120 million of the total 343 million doses of COVID-19 vaccines, were administered by retail pharmacies as of July 2021.[4])

Again, there was no worldwide public effort aimed at the public outcome of preventing disease and death. Instead, states and foreign governments engaged with private enterprises that used the public process to generate profit. Any public good was an intended and salutary side effect of all this activity—a good thing, but not what fired up the process. The net effect of the worldwide vaccination process so far has been huge private profit, wealth extraction from governments and communities around the world, and some public benefit, mostly in wealthy countries, which also retained the bulk of the wealth generated by this process. As a result, according to a *MarketWatch* head-line, "US wealth grew by $19 trillion during the pandemic—but mostly for the very rich."[5] Sounds like more colonialism to me.

But perhaps the most profound revelation brought by the pandemic (of the many revelations that the pandemic brought) was how effective medical colonialism has been at stripping neighborhoods and communities of their health agency, a revelation that was most clearly seen in vaccine hesitancy and refusal. At this writing, in February 2022, only about 75 percent of Americans have received one dose, 63 percent are fully vacci-nated, and 26 percent are fully vaccinated and boosted, more than one year after the vaccines became available and about eight months after they became widely available. Many people

of color and many white male Republicans have not been vaccinated and don't intend to be vaccinated, despite mountains of
evidence showing that the vaccines are effective and safe, are far
safer than contracting the virus, and are a very effective tool in
preventing hospitalizations and deaths, particularly when the
bulk of the population is vaccinated.

So why do people refuse an effective vaccine? The reasons
are many and varied: concerns about vaccine safety, concerns
about the speed at which vaccines were approved (paradox-
ically, by the FDA, an agency in the very government many
people profess to have lost faith in), mostly false beliefs about
the vaccine itself (such as beliefs that the vaccines involve an
implanted microchip, that the vaccines are Trump's way of killing off immigrants, or that the vaccines change a person's DNA
or will impair fertility), beliefs about individual freedom, and
concerns that the pandemic itself is a conspiracy created by the
vaccine manufacturers so that they could profit from vaccine
and booster sales—a belief that, while clearly not true, has a
certain basis in the activities and reputation for profit making
of those manufacturers.

There is tremendous pathos in vaccine hesitancy and
refusal, because many of the false beliefs have some basis both
in fact and in the experience of individuals and communities as
they have encountered health care in the US. But what no one
sees and no one knows is the way in which vaccine hesitancy and
refusal is the end product of a process that started many years
ago, when hospitals and insurance companies used their market
power to position themselves as the purveyors of health and
health services in the US; when Medicare and Medicaid began
to dominate how health services would be paid, making rules
that favored larger entities; when retail pharmacy chains first
pushed out local independent pharmacies and then entered the
market for vaccinations and many primary care services; and
when pharmaceutical companies made the vaccination business for-profit and then pivoted to finding and making drugs for
chronic disease. All these processes, combined, created a health

services marketplace in the US that pushed out local pharmacies and primary care physicians; made emergency rooms, hospitals, and insurance companies the places most people thought of when they thought of health care; made primary care physicians into employees; and disrupted the relationships of trust in health care that used to exist.

Once upon a time, many people sought health care from a local family physician who they knew and trusted and used a locally owned pharmacy where they were known and that they trusted as well. In those years, the notion of unself-interested advocacy—the idea that health professionals needed to put you and your interests first—defined the health care enterprise, and the relationship between patient and physician was primarily a relationship of trust, and often a relationship of love. In those years, your primary care physician would have called you and bugged you until you got vaccinated, and you would have listened, because you would have known and trusted that person. But medical colonialism and the culture of health care for profit intervened. Now few—just a little more than one-third of American adults—have a relationship with a primary care physician. The message from the market, which wanted to bust up that relationship so that it could sell you your vaccines and your treatment for a sore throat and your pregnancy test and so forth, is that you don't need a primary care physician and that you can get any information you need over the Internet. Information, perhaps, but not knowledge or wisdom, and not trust, and no relationship.

Now medicine is a for-profit enterprise. Many people sense that health care organizations have only profit as their motivation and that there is no longer anyone there to truly know people and communities as people and communities and to advocate for them, their health, and their lives. I hope this book will help others understand how accurate that perception has become. The locus of decision making about health is now in Washington or in corporate offices, not in people's homes or neighborhoods, and now many people, rightfully, don't trust anything the purveyors of health care as a business say or do.

Perversely, this for-profit process, which started out using health as a commodity that could be manufactured and sold, has made health impossible to achieve. The virus causes an infection. But medical colonialism and for-profit medicine—medicine as a business—caused the pandemic and all its associated illness, isolation, alienation, and death.

The only open question is whether we can look at what happened straight on and whether we can change, or if the power of the international corporate enterprise has become too great and will maintain its stranglehold on the health care enterprise into the foreseeable future—until medicine as colonialism causes the next pandemic, one that is worse and is so devastating as to force us to look at who we are and what our culture has become. If, by then, it is not too late.

CHAPTER ELEVEN

Final Thoughts, Summary and Conclusions, and a Little about How to Fix This Mess

O n the face of it, health care in the United States is a wreck beyond repair, a behemoth of private interests dedicated to private profit with no interest in the public's health beyond the ability to inflame people's fear of death and disability and marshal that fear to move product. The health care colonialists and profiteers use every lever at their disposal to keep the health care market as it is and to put their thumb on the scale of public policy so that they can do a better job of draining the public pocketbook. They've shanghaied the media, the airways, the Internet, the banks, our politics and our politicians, and even the health-care-purchasing apparatus of the military and the unions to extract money from people and communities and pour that money right into their own bank accounts. When they say, "Your money or your life," no one in our culture says, "How do we know that gun is loaded?" Or even, "Is that a real gun or just a toy?" Instead, we all say, "How much?" And even, "Was that enough?" Instead of banding together and taking our health care, our culture, and our nation back.

The extent of our colonization is remarkable. Once upon a time, we thought colonization happened to other countries, in underdeveloped places far away, places weakened by infighting, feudalism, and disease.

But in this book, I showed two things. First, we've seen how the leopard has changed its spots—that colonialism has changed and is no longer a force that only impacts distant nations. Instead, colonialization happens right here at home, as a multinational cabal of profiteers uses every lever at its disposal—military, government, international agencies, banks and other financial institutions, doctors, nurses, hospitals, community health centers, and insurance companies—to extract wealth from every community in the world, large and small, domestic and international, in our towns and neighborhoods in the US and in the barrios and villages of the developing world.

Second, we've learned that all our trusted health professionals and institutions are involved. Once upon a time, we thought of hospitals as places that care for the sick, of doctors as people who put the needs of their patients before their own interests, of nurses as angels who give endlessly of themselves, of researchers as people who work tirelessly for the good of all humanity, and even of insurance companies as organizations that resulted from people banding together to protect one another from the financial consequences of illness or injury. Now none of that is true. All health care professionals and organizations have been co-opted. The angels of our better nature have been poisoned. Most health care in the United States is made up of a troop of vampires who look like people we know, love, and trust but who are infected with greed and are here to drink our blood.

I can imagine only two pathways to fixing this mess, both extremely unlikely: either health professionals band together and go on strike, or we create a social movement like the civil rights movement, the antiwar movement, or the movement for marriage equality, in which communities take back their own health care, start providing health care for themselves, and then push the United States as a nation to assemble a real health care system that is for people and not for profit, so that we build a health care system that cares for all Americans cradle to grave and we build that health care system from the ground up.

It would be relatively easy for health care workers to go on strike without compromising the health of their patients or their communities, because most of the health care that exists today exists only for profit. Most doesn't impact the health of people or communities very much. Imagine a world in which we show up to work, listen to people who are sick, and treat them when they need treatment but also stop checking the boxes, filling out the forms, and sitting in front of the computers far into the night just to create the documentation one bureaucracy needs to bill another bureaucracy. Imagine us handwriting a medical record that we give to each patient to keep for themselves and handwriting prescriptions, choosing generic drugs to bring down the hegemony of Big Pharma. Just a tasty pipe dream for the legions of oppressed and disheartened health professionals, perhaps, but such a strike would force change. It would force governments to act. The folks with money would push back, of course, and might even start arresting us, but if we didn't back down, I think we would win, because they can't run their Medicare, Medicaid, and insurance-company dollar mills without us.

But we health professionals might have to give up our big cars, fancy houses, and weeks away hiking in the Himalayas or kayaking in Alaska or Puget Sound if such a strike happened, and before it led to a movement to create a health care system for the US. That lifestyle is why those of us who bemoan things as they are but make $200,000 to $400,000 a year and more are unlikely to strike—because we've been co-opted as well.

Creating a social movement to build a health care system for all Americans is also likely a pipe dream. It's a twenty- or thirty-year effort. We'd need people in every city and town, each building their own small health care system to care for their own neighbors and friends. We'd need statewide councils working to change state laws, which would have to engage in a pitched battle to beat back better-funded and well-organized coalitions of profiteers, who have proven their mettle when it comes to government affairs and who are able to use marketing, fake news, social media, lobbying, and bribery in order to subvert the public process. We'd need a national effort to change a ton of emmeshed law and bureaucracy in a government that can't seem to sort out who it actually exists to serve—the public good or "stakeholders" in bureaucracies that are themselves revolving doors, with their staff working for government one day and for industry the next—a government that seems to believe that its constituency is the lawyers and pundits who work on K Street in Washington, not the people who live and work just off Main Street and Broad Street in every city and town in the United States.

The smart money isn't called the smart money for nothing. They know how the game is played, and they know which side of the bread the butter lives on. It would take a huge social movement to change all that, people who are ready to march, to serve, and to act and not just post their bright ideas and emotions of the moment on Facebook, LinkedIn, and Instagram.

It took Simón Bolívar, Mahatma Gandhi, Ahmed Ben Bella, Amílcar Cabral, Che Guevara, Jomo Kenyatta, Patrice Lumumba, Kwame Nkrumah, Nelson Mandela, and many others years and tremendous sacrifice to throw off the yoke of the old colonial powers, but even as they did, those powers reinvented themselves and found myriad ways to continue to drain communities of their resources—and democracy, human rights, and social justice did not always replace the colonial governments that were kicked out.

It appears, then, that the path to social justice and democracy in health care is also not straight. But human life itself, the existence of any democracy, the presence of all human freedom, and the movement toward any social justice are all unlikely, but they occur anyway, alongside our fears and rational calculations, or perhaps in spite of those fears and calculations. Democracy is itself a process that involves struggle. Agency. Activation. And action.

It is not clear to me what path the evolution of health care in the United States will or must take. But it is clear that action and struggle make justice and democracy more likely. Hope exists in just that action and struggle, which gives both health care and human life meaning. We can watch and wait—and see the rich get richer while democracy collapses. Or we can stand up together, build health care systems that are for people, not for profit, and see if, by acting together, we can find that hidden, twisting, still-untrodden but liberating path.

Notes

ACKNOWLEDGMENTS
1   Wendell Berry, *Sex, Economy, Freedom & Community* (New York: Pantheon Books, 1993), 119–20.

FOREWORD
1   "Reported Cases, Deaths and Vaccinations by Country," *New York Times*, updated July 27, 2022, https://www.nytimes.com/interactive/2021/world/covid-cases.html.

INTRODUCTION
1   I was using vacation time from my employer during this period, and most of my time was volunteered and unpaid. When my vacation time ran out, I left that employer to work on this project full-time, all volunteer except for two hours a week that was part of a long-standing contract with one of the cities.

CHAPTER ONE **Medicine and Colonialism**
1   William H. Shrank, Teresa L. Rogstad, and Natasha Parekh, "Waste in the US Healthcare System: Estimated Costs and Potential for Savings," *JAMA* 322, no. 15 (October 7, 2019): 1501–09, https://doi.org/10.1001/jama.2019.13978.
2   Amanda Holpuch, "US Health Insurers Doubled Profits in Second Quarter amid Pandemic," *Guardian*, August 14, 2020, https://www.theguardian.com/us-news/2020/aug/14/us-health-insurers-coronavirus-pandemic-profit; "US Health Insurance Industry Analysis Report," National Association of Insurance Commissioners, accessed January 18, 2022, https://content.naic.org/sites/default/files/inline-files/2020-Annual-Health-Insurance-Industry-Analysis-Report.pdf.
3   Matej Mikulic, "Global Pharmaceutical Industry Statistics and Facts," *Statista*, September 10, 2021, https://www.statista.com/topics/1764/global-pharmaceutical-industry/.

CHAPTER TWO **Hospitals**

1   Centers for Disease Control and Prevention, "Achievements in Public Health, 1900-1999: Healthier Mothers and Babies," *MMWR* 48, no. 38 (October 1, 1999): 849–58, https://www.cdc.gov/mmwr/preview/mmwrhtml/mm4838a2. htm; Ignaz Semmelweis, "The Aetiology, Concept and Prophylaxis of Puerperal Fever," *Med Classics* 5 (1941): 350; Sherry L. Murphy, Kenneth D. Kochanek, Jiaquan Xu, and Elizabeth Arias, "Mortality in the United States, 2020," National Center for Health Statistics Data Brief, no. 427, December 2021, https://dx.doi.org/10.15620/cdc:112079.

2   Lucinda Shen, "These Are the 21 Largest Endowments and Foundations in the US," *Business Insider*, September 11, 2015, https://www.businessinsider. com/20-largest-us-endowments-and-foundations-2015-9.

3   "Top 40 Largest Healthcare Foundation Rankings by Total Assets," Sovereign Wealth Fund Institute, accessed February 4, 2022, https://www.swfinstitute. org/fund-rankings/healthcare-foundation.

4   "National Health Expenditures 2020 Highlights," Centers for Medicaid and Medicaid Services, accessed January 23, 2022, https://www.cms.gov/files/ document/highlights.pdf.

5   HRSA, the Health Resources and Services Administration, does identify shortage areas, called Health Professional Shortage Areas, for primary care physicians, nurse-practitioners, physician assistants, dentists, psychiatrists, and a few other disciplines. The process for doing so, however, is arcane and subject to lots of political manipulation—and the process for addressing those needs is obscure and entirely voluntary. No one figures out where the needs are greatest, trains up the needed health professionals, and then locates them in those areas of greatest need in any coherent or consistent fashion.

6   "Hospitals," Data USA, accessed May 30, 2021, https://datausa.io/profile/ naics/hospitals#workforce.

7   Adam Andrzejewski, "Top US 'Non-Profit' Hospitals & CEOs Are Racking Up Huge Profits," *Forbes*, June 26, 2019, https://www.forbes.com/sites/ adamandrzejewski/2019/06/26/top-u-s-non-profit-hospitals-ceos-are- racking-up-huge-profits/?sh=4cf205f919df.

8   Frederic Michas, "Number of Hospital Employees in the U.S. 2004–2018," *Statista*, November 18, 2020, https://www.statista.com/statistics/632385/ hospital-staff-part-time-full-time/; Earlene Dowell, "Census Bureau's 2018 County Business Patterns Provides Data on Over 1,200 Industries," United States Census Bureau, October 14, 2020, https://www.census.gov/library/ stories/2020/10/health-care-still-largest-united-states-employer.html.

9   Steffie Woolhandler, Terry Campbell, and David U. Himmelstein, "Costs of Healthcare Administration in the United States and Canada," *New England Journal of Medicine* 349 (2003): 768–75, https://www.nejm.org/doi/full/10.1056/ nejmsa022033.

10   "Emergency Department Visits," National Center of Health Statistics, Centers for Disease Control and Prevention, last reviewed March 25, 2022, https:// www.cdc.gov/nchs/fastats/emergency-department.htm.

11   The aggressive debt collection practices of hospitals are well known and have been widely documented.

12   Chris Pomorski, "The Death of Hahnemann Hospital," *New Yorker*, May 31, 2021, https://www.newyorker.com/magazine/2021/06/07/the-death-of-hahnemann-hospital.

13   Ayla Ellison, "Steward, Medical Billing Company Accused of Illegal 'Revenue Enhancement' Scheme," *Becker's Hospital CFO Report*, August 11, 2020, https://www.beckershospitalreview.com/finance/steward-medical-billing-company-accused-of-illegal-revenue-enhancement-scheme.html; United States Department of Justice, "Prime Healthcare Services and CEO to Pay $65 Million to Settle False Claims Act Allegations," press release no. 18-1014, August 3, 2018, https://www.justice.gov/opa/pr/prime-healthcare-services-and-ceo-pay-65-million-settle-false-claims-act-allegations.

14   Steven Fiorillo, "Medical Properties Trust: Yielding 5% while Growing Revenue and FFO," *Seeking Alpha*, December 17, 2021, https://seekingalpha.com/article/4475517-medical-properties-trust-yielding-5-percent-while-growing-revenue-and-ffo; Jussi Askola, "Why I Doubled Down on Medical Properties Trust," *Seeking Alpha*, January 11, 2022, https://seekingalpha.com/article/4478663-why-i-doubled-down-on-medical-properties-trust. The latter writer groups the ownership of hospitals with the ownership of casinos as the best available real estate investments.

15   Brian Spegele and Laura Cooper, "PE-Backed Hospital Chain Got Help from Major Landlord as Losses Mounted," *Wall Street Journal*, June 18, 2021, https://www.wsj.com/articles/pe-backed-hospital-chain-got-help-from-major-landlord-as-losses-mounted-11624014000.

16   In addition to the direct payments from Medicare, Medicaid, the VA, and public employee insurance, hospitals receive 20 to 30 percent of their income from health insurance companies. But since employers' insurance costs are tax-deductible expenses, a portion of those insurance payments, likely 20 to 30 percent, are effective tax subsidies for employers, and so that portion represents further government funding of hospitals.

CHAPTER THREE Pharma and Pharmaceutical Retailers

1   Substance Abuse and Mental Health Services Administration, *Key Substance Use and Mental Health Indicators in the United States: Results from the 2019 National Survey on Drug Use and Health*, HHS Pub. No. PEP20-07-01-001, NSDUH Series H-55 (2020), https://www.samhsa.gov/data/sites/default/files/reports/rpt2 9393/2019NSDUHFFRPDFWHTML/2019NSDUHFFR090120.htm.

2   Substance Abuse and Mental Health Services Administration, *Key Substance Use and Mental Health Indicators*.

3   Art Van Zee, "The Promotion and Marketing of OxyContin: Commercial Triumph, Public Health Tragedy," *American Journal of Public Health* 99, no. 2 (February 2009): 221–27, https://doi.org/10.2105/AJPH.2007.131714.

4   Hilary Aroke, Ashley Buchanan, Xuerong Wen, Peter Ragosta, Jennifer Koziol, and Stephen Kogut, "Estimating the Direct Costs of Outpatient

Opioid Prescriptions: A Retrospective Analysis of Data from the Rhode Island Prescription Drug Monitoring Program," *Journal of Managed Care & Specialty Pharmacy* 24, no. 3 (March 2018), 214–24, https://doi.org/10.18553/jmcp.2018.24.3.214.

5   US Department of Health and Human Services Office of the Inspector General, "Opioids in Medicare Part D: Concerns about Extreme Use and Questionable Prescribing," data brief no. OEI-02-17-00250, July 2017, https://oig.hhs.gov/oei/reports/oei-02-17-00250.pdf.

6   Katherine Young and Julia Zur, "Medicaid and the Opioid Epidemic: Enrollment, Spending, and the Implications of Proposed Policy Changes," Kaiser Family Foundation, July 14, 2017, https://www.kff.org/medicaid/issue-brief/medicaid-and-the-opioid-epidemic-enrollment-spending-and-the-implications-of-proposed-policy-changes/.

7   "Prescription Drug Spending in the U.S. Healthcare System," American Academy of Actuaries, March 2018, https://www.actuary.org/content/prescription-drug-spending-us-health-care-system; "A Look at Drug Spending in the U.S.: Estimates and Projections from Various Stakeholders," Pew Charitable Trust, February 27, 2018, https://www.pewtrusts.org/en/research-and-analysis/fact-sheets/2018/02/a-look-at-drug-spending-in-the-us.

8   Samantha McGrail, "Fundamentals of the Pharmacy Supply Chain," *PharmaNews Intelligence*, July 1, 2020, https://pharmanewsintel.com/news/fundamentals-of-the-pharmaceutical-supply-chain.

9   Nathan Bomey, "CVS to Help Underserved Americans Schedule COVID-19 Vaccine Appointments," USA Today, February 21, 2021, https://www.usatoday.com/story/money/2021/02/19/covid-vaccine-appointments-cvs-pharmacy-coronavirus/6787649002/.

10   J. Scott Ashwood, Martin Gaynor, Claude M. Setodji, Rachel O. Reid, Ellerie Weber, and Ateev Mehrotra, "Retail Clinic Visits for Low-Acuity Conditions Increase Utilization and Spending," *Health Affairs* 35, no. 3 (March 2016): 449–55, https://doi.org/10.1377/hlthaff.2015.0995.

11   Scott Howell, Perry T. Yin, and James C. Robinson, "Quantifying the Economic Burden of Drug Utilization Management on Payers, Manufacturers, Physicians, and Patients," *Health Affairs* 40, no. 8 (August 2021): 1206–14, https://doi.org/10.1377/hlthaff.2021.00036.

12   "List of U.S. State Budgets," Wikipedia, accessed July 25, 2022, https://en.wikipedia.org/wiki/List_of_U.S._state_budgets.

13   Zach Stanley, "How Many Pharma Companies Are in the Fortune Top 50? Guess Again," *MassBio News*, February 12, 2019, https://www.massbio.org/news/recent-news/how-many-pharma-companies-are-in-the-fortune-top-50-guess-again/.

14   Michael Fine, *Health Care Revolt: How to Organize, Build a Health Care System, and Resuscitate Democracy—All at the Same Time* (Oakland: PM Press, 2018), 49–52.

CHAPTER FOUR Specialists, Surgicenters, Radiologists, Cardiologists, and Tests

1   Brian D. Smedley, Adrienne Y. Stith, and Alan R. Nelson, eds., *Unequal Treatment: Confronting Racial and Ethnic Disparities in Health Care* (Washington, DC: The National Academies Press, 2003), https://doi.org/10.17226/12875.

2   "Revenue of U.S. Medical Schools by Source, Fiscal Year 2020," Association of American Medical Colleges, accessed June 23, 2021, https://www.aamc.org/data-reports/interactive-data/i-revenue-us-medical-schools-source-fiscal-year-2021.

3   "National Ambulatory Medical Care Survey: 2015 State and National Summary Tables," Centers for Disease Control and Prevention, National Center for Health Statistics, 1, 13, 18, accessed June 24, 2022, https://www.cdc.gov/nchs/data/ahcd/namcs_summary/2015_namcs_web_tables.pdf.

CHAPTER FIVE Administrators, Consultants, Lawyers, and Doctors

1   Kimberly Amadeo, "The Rising Cost of Health Care by Year and Its Causes," *The Balance*, March 26, 2016, https://www.thebalance.com/causes-of-rising-healthcare-costs-4064878.

2   Aaron C. Catlin and Cathy A. Cowan, "History of Health Spending in the United States, 1960–2013," Centers for Medicare and Medicaid Services, November 19, 2015, https://www.cms.gov/Research-Statistics-Data-and-Systems/Statistics-Trends-and-Reports/NationalHealthExpendData/Downloads/HistoricalNHEPaper.pdf.

3   David Rothman, *Strangers at the Bedside: A History of How Law and Bioethics Transformed Medical Decision Making* (New York: Basic Books, 1992).

4   David U. Himmelstein, Terry Campbell, and Steffie Woolhandler, "Healthcare Administrative Costs in the United States and Canada, 2017," *Annals of Internal Medicine* 172, no. 2 (January 21, 2020): 134–42, https://doi.org/10.7326/M19-2818.

5   Nisha Kurani, Jared Ortaliza, Emma Wager, Lucas Fox, and Krutika Amin, "How Has U.S. Spending on Healthcare Changed over Time?" *Petersen-KFF Health System Tracker*, December 23, 2020, https://www.healthsystemtracker.org/chart-collection/u-s-spending-healthcare-changed-time/#item-usspendingovertime_14.

6   David M. Cutler, "The Good and Bad News of Healthcare Employment," *JAMA* 319, no. 8 (2018): 758–59, https://doi.org/:10.1001/jama.2018.1054 (emphasis added).

7   Laura Tollen, Elizabeth Keating, and Alan Weil, "How Administrative Spending Contributes to Excess US Health Spending," *Health Affairs*, February 20, 2020, https://www.healthaffairs.org/do/10.1377/forefront.20200218.375060/full/.

8   Alexa Gagosz, "R.I. Agreed to Pay Consulting Firm $12.4m to Help with Covid-19 Response," *Boston Globe*, February 5, 2021, https://www.bostonglobe.com/2021/02/05/metro/ri-agreed-pay-consulting-firm-124m-help-with-covid-19-response/.

9   Michelle M. Mello, Amitabh Chandra, Atul A. Gawande, and David M. Studdert, "National Costs of the Medical Liability System," *Health Affairs* 29, no. 9 (September 2010): 1569–77, https://doi.org/10.1377/hlthaff.2009.0807.

CHAPTER SIX Primary Care

1   Lauren Wilbert, "MinuteClinic Moving to CVS Pharmacy," *Minneapolis/St. Paul Business Journal*, May 8, 2006, https://www.bizjournals.com/twincities/stories/2006/05/08/daily1.html.
2   Sandra G. Boodman, "For Millennials, a Regular Visit to the Doctor Is Not a Primary Concern," *Washington Post*, October 6, 2018, https://www.washingtonpost.com/national/health-science/for-millennials-a-regular-visit-to-the-doctors-office-is-not-a-primary-concern/2018/10/05/6b17c71a-aef3-11e8-9a6a-565d92a3585d_story.html.

CHAPTER SEVEN Insurance Companies

1   Paul Starr, *The Social Transformation of American Medicine* (New York: Basic Books, 1982), 235–310.
2   Mark A. Hall and Christopher J. Conover, "The Impact of Blue Cross Conversions on Accessibility, Affordability, and the Public Interest," *Milbank Quarterly* 81, no. 4 (December 16, 2003): 509–42, https://doi.org/10.1046/j.0887-378X.2003.00293.x.
3   "Options to Reduce State Medicaid Costs Managed Care: Medical Loss Ratio," Center on Budget and Policy Priorities, August 31, 2020, https://www.cbpp.org/research/health/options-to-reduce-state-medicaid-costs-managed-care-medical-loss-ratio.
4   "Medicaid Per Capita Expenditures," Centers for Medicare and Medicaid Services, accessed July 1, 2021, https://www.medicaid.gov/stateoverviews/scorecard/how-much-states-spend-per-medicaid-enrollee/index.html.
5   "Primary Care Investment," Primary Care Collaborative, accessed July 1, 2021, https://www.pcpcc.org/primary-care-investment.

CHAPTER EIGHT Research

1   "Top 200 Science Cities" Nature Index, Supplements, accessed July 8, 2021, https://www.natureindex.com/supplements/nature-index-2018-science-cities/tables/overall.
2   "How Much Does a Scientist Make in the United States?" Salary.com, accessed June 27, 2022, https://www1.salary.com/Scientist-Salary.html.
3   "Scientists and Engineers Working in Science and Engineering Occupations in 2015" (chart), National Science Foundation, Women, Minorities, and Persons with Disabilities in Science and Engineering, accessed July 8, 2021, https://www.nsf.gov/statistics/2017/nsf17310/digest/occupation/overall.cfm.
4   José J. Escarce and Kanika Kapur, "Racial and Ethnic Differences in Public and Private Medical Care Expenditures among Aged Medicare Beneficiaries," *Milbank Quarterly* 81, no. 2 (June 6, 2003): 249–75, https://doi.org/10.1111/1468-0009.t01-1-00053.

5   Mary A. Garza, Sandra Crouse Quinn, Yan Li, Luciana Assini-Meytin, Erica T. Casper, Craig S. Fryer, James Butler III, Natasha A. Brown, Kevin H. Kim, and Stephen B. Thomas, "The Influence of Race and Ethnicity on Becoming a Human Subject: Factors Associated with Participation in Research," *Contemporary Clinical Trials Communications* 7 (September 2017): 57–63, https://doi.org/10.1016/j.conctc.2017.05.009; Patrick S. Sullivan, A.D. McNaghten, Elin Begley, Angela Hutchinson, and Victoria A. Cargill, "Enrollment of Racial/Ethnic Minorities and Women with HIV in Clinical Research Studies of HIV Medicines," *Journal of the National Medical Association* 99, no. 3 (March 2007): 242; Stacie E. Geller, Abby Koch, Beth Pellettieri, and Molly Carnes, "Inclusion, Analysis, and Reporting of Sex and Race/Ethnicity in Clinical Trials: Have We Made Progress?" *Journal of Women's Health* 20, no.3 (March 2011): 315–20, https://doi.org/10.1089/jwh.2010.2469; Vivek H. Murthy, Harlan M. Krumholz, and Cary P. Gross, "Participation in Cancer Clinical Trials: Race-, Sex-, and Age-Based Disparities," *JAMA* 291, no. 22 (June 2004): 2720–26, https://doi.org/10.1001/jama.291.22.2720.

6   "The Tuskegee Timeline," Centers for Disease Control and Prevention, U.S. Public Health Service Syphilis Study at Tuskegee, accessed July 9, 2021, https://www.cdc.gov/tuskegee/timeline.htm.

7   Rebecca Skloot, *The Immortal Life of Henrietta Lacks* (New York: Broadway Paperbacks, 2011).

8   Rebecca Robbins, "Most Experimental Drugs Are Tested Offshore—Raising Concerns about Data," *Scientific American*, September 10, 2017, https://www.scientificamerican.com/article/most-experimental-drugs-are-tested-offshore-raising-concerns-about-data/.

9   Jennifer E. Miller, Michelle M. Mello, Joshua D. Wallach, et al., "Evaluation of Drug Trials in High-, Middle-, and Low-Income Countries and Local Commercial Availability of Newly Approved Drugs," *JAMA Network Open* 4, no. 5 (May 5, 2021), https://doi.org/10.1001/jamanetworkopen.2021.7075.

10 "Domestic and International Revenue of the U.S. Pharmaceutical Industry between 1975 and 2020," *Statista*, September 15, 2021, https://www.statista.com/statistics/275560/domestic-and-international-revenue-of-the-us-pharmaceutical-industry/.

11 "Coronavirus (COVID-19) Vaccinations," Our World in Data, accessed August 12, 2021, https://ourworldindata.org/covid-vaccinations.

CHAPTER NINE Medical Colonialism as, Well, Colonialism Itself

1   Jan Ascher, Boris Bogdan, Julio Dreszer, and Gaobo Zhou, "Pharma's Next Challenge," McKinsey and Company, July 1, 2015, https://www.mckinsey.com/industries/life-sciences/our-insights/pharmas-next-challenge.

2   "Accelerating Access in Emerging Markets: Pharma's Next Big Launch Challenge," McKinsey and Company, accessed January 28, 2022, https://www.mckinsey.com/~/media/McKinsey/Industries/Pharmaceuticals%20and%20Medical%20Products/Our%20Insights/Pharmas%20next%20challenge/Pharmas_next_challenge.ashx.

3   Maya Tannoury and Zouhair Attieh, "The Influence of Emerging Markets on the Pharmaceutical Industry," *Current Therapeutic Research* 86 (2017): 19–22, https://doi.org/10.1016/j.curtheres.2017.04.005.

4   Edward Baer, "Babies Mean Business," *New Internationalist*, April 1982, https://newint.org/features/1982/04/01/babies.

5   Arthur Neslen, "Nestlé under Fire for Marketing Claims on Baby Milk Formulas," *Guardian*, February 1, 2018, https://www.theguardian.com/business/2018/feb/01/nestle-under-fire-for-marketing-claims-on-baby-milk-formulas.

6   George Kent, "Global Infant Formula: Monitoring and Regulating the Impacts to Protect Human Health," *International Breastfeeding Journal* 10 (February 23, 2015): 6, https://doi.org/10.1186/s13006-014-0020-7.

7   Anna Gilmore, "Big Tobacco Targets the Young in Poor Countries—with Deadly Consequences," *The Guardian*, December 1, 2015, https://www.theguardian.com/global-development/2015/dec/01/big-tobacco-industry-targets-young-people-poor-countries-smoking.

8   Paul Lendner and Lola Butcher, "Medical Tourism: Once Ready for Takeoff, Now Stuck at the Gate," Managedcaremag.com, March 26, 2021, https://www.managedcaremag.com/archives/2018/4/medical-tourism-once-ready-takeoff-now-stuck-gate/.

9   Awad A. Ahmed, Wei-Ting Hwang, Charles R. Thomas Jr., and Curtiland Deville Jr., "International Medical Graduates in the US Physician Workforce and Graduate Medical Education: Current and Historical Trends," *Journal of Graduate Medical Education* 10, no. 2 (April 2018): 214–18, https://pubmed.ncbi.nlm.nih.gov/29686763/; "How IMGs Have Changed the Face of American Medicine," American Medical Association, October 19, 2021, https://www.ama-assn.org/education/international-medical-education/how-imgs-have-changed-face-american-medicine.

10   Linda H. Aiken, "U.S. Nurse Labor Market Dynamics Are Key to Global Nurse Sufficiency," *Health Services Research* 42, no. 3 part 2 (June 2007): 1299–1320, https://doi.org/10.1111/j.1475-6773.2007.00714.x.

11   Steve Dubb, "Cuban Medical School Trains US Doctors of Color," *Nonprofit Quarterly*, June 8, 2018, https://nonprofitquarterly.org/cuban-medical-school-trains-us-primary-care-doctors-of-color.

12   The percentage is likely smaller, according to a very senior faculty member who wishes to remain anonymous. The Association of American Medical Colleges lists the number of medical students in Rhode Island who matriculate in state at 28 percent, but it doesn't explicate its methodology for arriving at that finding. Brown is Rhode Island's only medical school. But many Brown medical students went to Brown because of Brown's Program in Liberal Medical Education (PLME), an eight-year program that combines undergraduate studies and medical school, so many become Rhode Island residents before matriculating. A more accurate representation would be the percent of matriculating medical students who went to high school in Rhode Island, but no such publicly available number exists. See "Rhode Island

Physician Workforce Projections 2019–2020," AAMC, accessed January 30, 2022, https://www.aamc.org/media/58316/download.

CHAPTER TEN COVID-19

1   "Coronavirus (COVID-19) Vaccinations," Our World in Data, accessed July 23, 2021, https://ourworldindata.org/covid-vaccinations.

2   Steve Eder, Henry Fountain, Michael H. Keller, Muyi Xiao, and Alexandra Stevenson, "430,000 People Have Traveled from China to U.S. Since Coronavirus Surfaced," *New York Times*, April 5, 2020, https://www.nytimes.com/2020/04/04/us/coronavirus-china-travel-restrictions.html; Najmul Haider, Alexei Yavlinsky, David Simons, et al., "Passengers' Destinations from China: Low Risk of Novel Coronavirus (2019-nCoV) Transmission into Africa and South America," *Epidemiology & Infection* 148 (February 26, 2020): e41, https://doi.org/10.1017/S0950268820000424.

3   "Combatting COVID-19: Reflections from the Field on Vaccine Distribution," Alvarez & Marsal, Public Sector Services, accessed July 28, 2021, https://www.alvarezandmarsal.com/sites/default/files/pss_combatting_covid_19_apr_2021.pdf; "COVID-19 Vaccine Distribution: Are You Ready?" John Snow, Inc., accessed July 28, 2021, https://www.jsi.com/preparing-for-covid-19-vaccine-distribution/.

4   "The Federal Retail Pharmacy Program for COVID-19 Vaccination," Centers for Disease Control and Prevention, COVID-19 Vaccination, Planning & Partnerships, accessed July 28, 2021, https://www.cdc.gov/vaccines/covid-19/retail-pharmacy-program/; Tom Randall, Cedric Sam, Andre Tartar, Paul Murray, and Christopher Cannon, "More Than 10.2 Billion Shots Given: Covid-19 Tracker," *Bloomberg*, accessed July 28, 2021, https://www.bloomberg.com/graphics/covid-vaccine-tracker-global-distribution/n/.

5   Joy Wiltermuth, "U.S. Wealth Grew by $19 Trillion during the Pandemic—But Mostly for the Very Rich," *MarketWatch*, July 27, 2021, https://www.marketwatch.com/story/u-s-wealth-grew-by-19-trillion-during-the-pandemic-but-mostly-for-the-very-rich-11627428603.

Bibliography

Berry, Wendell. *Sex, Economy, Freedom & Community*. New York: Pantheon Books, 1993.

Bishop, Bill. *The Big Sort: Why the Clustering of Like-Minded America Is Tearing Us Apart*. Boston: Houghton Mifflin, 2008.

Brownlee, Shannon. *Overtreated: Why Too Much Medicine Is Making Us Sicker and Poorer*. New York: Bloomsbury, 2007.

Donaldson, Molla, Karl Yordy, Kathleen Lohr, and Neal Vanselow, eds. *Primary Care: American's Health in a New Era*. Washington, DC: National Academy Press, 1966.

Dubos, René. *Mirage of Health: Utopias, Progress, and Biological Change*. New Brunswick, NJ: Rutgers University Press, 1996.

Fine, Michael. *Health Care Revolt: How to Organize, Build a Health Care System, and Resuscitate Democracy—All at the Same Time*. Oakland: PM Press, 2018.

Illich, Ivan. *Medical Nemesis: The Expropriation of Health*. New York: Pantheon Books, 1982.

Kleinke, J.D. *Oxymorons: The Myth of a U.S. Health Care System*. San Francisco: Jossey-Bass, 2001.

Kotelchuck, David, ed. *Prognosis Negative: Crisis in the Health Care System*. New York: Vintage Books, 1976.

Mahar, Maggie. *Money-Driven Medicine: The Real Reason Health Care Costs So Much*. New York: Collins, 2006.

Mullan, Fitzhugh. *White Coat, Clenched Fist: The Political Education of an American Physician*. Ann Arbor: University of Michigan Press, 2006.

Putnam, Robert. *Bowling Alone: The Collapse and Revival of American Community*. New York: Simon & Schuster, 2000.

Rawls, John. *A Theory of Justice*. Cambridge, MA: Belknap Press, 1971.

Rosenthal, Elisabeth. *An American Sickness: How Healthcare Became Big Business and How You Can Take It Back*. New York: Penguin Press, 2017.

Rothman, David. *Strangers at the Bedside: A History of How Law and Bioethics Transformed Medical Decision Making*. New York: Basic Books, 1992.

Skloot, Rebecca. *The Immortal Life of Henrietta Lacks*. New York: Broadway Paperbacks, 2011.

Smedley, Brian D., Adrienne Y. Stith, and Alan R. Nelson, eds. *Unequal Treatment: Confronting Racial and Ethnic Disparities in Health Care.* Washington, DC: National Academies Press, 2003. https://doi.org/10.17226/12875.

Starfield, Barbara. *Primary Care: Balancing Health Needs, Services and Technology.* New York: Oxford University Press, 1998.

Starr, Paul. *The Social Transformation of American Medicine.* New York: Basic Books, 1982.

Stevens, Rosemary. *American Medicine and the Public Interest: A History of Specialization.* Berkeley: University of California Press, 1971.

———. *In Sickness and in Wealth: American Hospitals in the Twentieth Century.* New York: Basic Books, 1989.

Index

"Passim" (literally "scattered") indicates intermittent discussion of a topic over a cluster of pages.

actuaries and actuarial work, 91
administrative cost of health care, 69–70, 72
advertising: emergency departments, 28; opiates, 37
Affordable Care Act, 49, 84, 86
African Americans: COVID-19, vii; ELAM, 121; infant mortality and life expectancy, 57; scientists, 98–99; war on drugs, 36–37; Washington, DC, 29
Alvarez & Marsal, 71, 128
Amazon, 76
antitrust law immunity, 89–90
Apollo Global Management, 29, 30

back pain, 11, 28, 37
billers and billing, 68; hospitals, 27, 32
Black, Eli, 29
Black, Leon, 29
Black Americans. See African Americans
blood pressure, high. See hypertension
Blue Cross, 83
Blue Cross Blue Shield, 85
breastfeeding, 115
Brown University, 121, 144n12

cadavers, 60–61, 118
Centers for Medicare and Medicaid Services (CMS), 27
Central Falls, Rhode Island, 8, 68–69; COVID-19, 1–5, 70–71, 93–94
CEO pay: hospitals, 12, 24
Cerberus Capital, 30, 33
chain drugstores. See drugstore chains
charitably funded hospitals, 19, 31
childbirth mortality, 17–18
China, 114; COVID-19, 124–27 passim
chronic disease, 38, 39–40, 41, 108–9; COVID-19 and, 79. See also hypertension
Civil Rights Act of 1964, 22
clinical trials, 52–53, 94–96, 102–3, 111
clinics, pharmacy-based. See pharmacy-based clinics
collusion: health insurers, 89
"colonialism" (word), 11–14 passim
community health centers, 8, 46, 59, 68–69, 76; COVID-19 vaccine, 78
consultants, 4, 70–71
Council on Graduate Medical Education, 61, 63

COVID-19, vii, ix, 124–31; Central Falls and Pawtucket, R.I., 1–5, 70–71, 93–94; conspiracy theories, 129; people of color, vii; research, 104; super-spreader events, 126–27; testing, 45; vaccines and vaccination, 78–79, 89, 93–94, 104, 111, 124–29

CT scans, 28, 31, 59

Cuba, 120–21

CVS, 44, 45, 47, 76, 127, 128

De la Torre, Ralph, 33

Depression. See Great Depression

diabetes, 39–40, 106–8

diagnostic testing, 11, 28, 31, 59

"doctors' hospitals," 18–19

donated bodies. See cadavers

drug addiction (prescription drugs). See prescription drug addiction

drug industry, 36–53, 103; clinical trials, 103; profits, 12, 49; tobacco addiction and, 116; world market, 103, 108–14 passim, 123

drug overdose death (prescription drugs). See overdose death (prescription drugs)

drugs, 41–42; clinical trials, 52–53, 94–96, 102–3, 111; dispensing, 50–51; group purchasing, 49; lawsuits, 72; patent rights and protection, 51, 104–5, 110–11, 119; per person annual spending, 41, 43; prices, 40, 42, 43, 110; production cost, 43; research and development, 43, 48–49, 51–52, 110, 111; sales worldwide, 103, 108–10; for tobacco addiction, 116. See also generic drugs; opiates; orphan drugs

drugstore chains, 40–41, 43, 44–45, 46, 50, 76; COVID-19 vaccination and, 127–28

Dubb, Steve, 120–21

Ebola, 119

ELAM (Escuela Latinoamericana de Medicina), 120–21

Emergency Medical Treatment and Labor Act of 1986 (EMTALA), 10–11

emergency departments (ERs), 20, 28, 56, 62–63, 64

employers: Blue Cross and, 83; employer-purchased health insurance, 90, 139n16; paycheck deductions, 60; workers' compensation, 82–83

epidemics: Ebola, 119; opiate overdose deaths, 72

family practice, 75, 80, 130

fentanyl, 37

flu shots, 77, 78

food, 43, 48, 53; fast food, 109

Food and Drug Administration (FDA), 49, 103, 129

foreign workforce, 117–19

fraud in hospital billing, 32

Freedman, Joel, 29–30

generic drugs, 40, 49, 50, 110, 111, 122, 123, 134

globalization (economics), 112

government employee health insurance. See public employee health insurance

Great Depression, 82–83

guinea pigs (human volunteers). See medical research subjects

Hahnemann University Hospital, Philadelphia, 29–30

health care services, unnecessary. See unnecessary health care services

health care spending, 12, 23, 67–69 passim, 108; consultants, 71; drugs, 41–44 passim; Medicaid, 88; opioid addiction, 38

health care workforce: developing
world as source for, 117–19;
Health Professional Shortage
Areas, 138n5; hypothetical strike,
133
health insurance, people without.
See uninsured people
health insurance, public employee.
See public employee health
insurance
health insurers, 26, 27, 43–44, 50,
56, 82–92; drug companies and,
40–41; lobbying, 50; Medicaid
and, 57; medical tourism, 117;
nonprofit, 85; PBMs and, 47;
profits, 12
Health Resources and Services
Administration (HRSA), 61, 138n5
heart disease, 39–40
hedge funds, 14, 31–34 passim, 76,
88, 90
HIV research, 104; Kenya, 102
Hospital Corporation of America, 19
hospitals, 9, 17–35, 54–57 passim,
82, 89–90, 139n16; billing, 27,
32; CEO pay, 12, 24; closing, 2, 9,
30, 31, 34; governing boards, 21;
insurance, 82–83; lobbying, 24,
26; Medicaid and, 87; medical
school funding, 6. *See also*
"doctors' hospitals"; teaching
hospitals; university hospitals
human experimentation. *See* clinical
trials; medical research subjects
hypertension, 39–40; medications,
51

infant formula, 115–16
infant mortality, 17, 57, 59, 122;
Liberia, 119
informed consent, 52–53, 94–96, 99,
100
institutional review boards (IRBs),
52, 97, 103

insurance companies. *See* health
insurers
intellectual property, 52, 110–13
passim, 120

John Snow, Inc., 71, 128
Joint Commission, 37

Kent, George, 116
Kenya: hemoglobin A1c machine
and diabetes diagnostics, 106–8;
HIV research, 102
kickbacks and side deals. *See*
sweetheart deals

Lacks, Henrietta, 101
Latin American School of Medicine,
Cuba. *See* ELAM (Escuela
Latinoamericana de Medicina)
Latinos: COVID-19, vii; ELAM, 121;
scientists, 98–99; war on drugs,
36–37
lawsuits: drug companies, 72;
malpractice, 73, 76
lawyers, 68, 72–73, 114
Liberia, 119, 121
life expectancy, 17, 41, 51, 57, 59, 67,
122; Liberia, 119
lobbying, 46; Blue Cross, 83;
consultants, 71; drug industry, 49,
114; health insurers, 50; hospitals,
24, 26; specialists, 63
Local Initiatives Support
Corporation (LISC), 4

malpractice, 73
maternal mortality, 17–18
McCarran-Ferguson Act of 1954,
89–90
McKinsey and Company, 109–10
Medicaid, 9, 15, 19–21 passim, 34,
43, 47, 65, 86–88; actuarial work,
91; fraudulent billing and, 32;
group drug purchasing, 49;
history, 86; hospital physicians'

payments, 60; "managed care" (private insurers and), 57; opioid addiction and, 38; orthopedic care and, 55–56; psychiatric care and, 57, 63; specialists and, 61
medical consultants. *See* consultants
medical education. *See* medical school
medical journals, 37, 96, 123
Medical Properties Trust, 33
"medical research centers," 97
medical research subjects, 52–53, 94–102 passim
medical residents. *See* residents and residency
medical schools and medical education, 59–61, 63; Brown University, 121, 144n12; Cuba, 120–21; developing world, 117–19 passim
medical specialists. *See* specialists and specialty care
medical tourism, 117
Medicare, 9, 15, 19–21 passim, 26–27, 34, 43, 47, 65, 86–88; actuarial work, 91; Advantage plan, 87, 88; Civil Rights Act of 1964 and, 22; Congress and, 86; fraudulent billing and, 32; group drug purchasing, 49; history, 86; hospital physicians' payments, 60; Part D (prescriptions), 38; psychiatric care and, 57, 63; residency and, 30, 61; specialists and, 61
MidCap Financial, 29, 30
MinuteClinic, 76
money laundering, 33
monopolies: pharmacists, 46, 50; specialists, 63
MRIs, 11, 28, 31
multinational corporations, 13, 113

National Institutes of Health (NIH), 51, 52, 96

Nestlé: infant formula marketing, 116, 117
New Orleans, 54–55
nonprofit health insurance companies. *See* health insurers: nonprofit
nurses: foreign-educated, 118, 119; pay, 24; as percentage of health care workers, 69; speedup, 32

Obama, Barack, 49
Obamacare. *See* Affordable Care Act
Ochsner Medical Center, New Orleans, 54–55, 57
1Life Healthcare, 76
opiates: overdose deaths, 72; prescription and addiction, 37
orphan drugs, 49
orthopedists and orthopedics, 55–56
out-of-pocket health care spending, 67
overdose death (prescription drugs), 36, 37–38, 72
overtesting and overtreatment. *See* unnecessary health care services

pain, 11, 28, 37; treatment, 37
Paladin Healthcare Capital, 29–30
pandemics, 39, 41, 120. *See also* COVID-19
patent rights and protection, 51, 104–5, 108–13 passim, 119
Patient Protection and Affordable Care Act. *See* Affordable Care Act
Pawtucket, Rhode Island, 8; COVID-19, 2–5
pay, hospital workers', 24–25, 55
pharmaceutical industry. *See* drug industry
pharmacy-based clinics, 76, 77–78
pharmacy benefit managers (PBMs), 47–48, 49
pharmacy chains. *See* drugstore chains

Philadelphia, 29–30
placebos, 95, 99
polio, 104
prescription drug addiction and
  overdose, 36, 37–38
prescription drugs, *See* drugs
primary care and primary care
  physicians, 25–26, 58–68 passim,
  75–81, 89; health insurers and, 84;
  Medicaid and, 87
Prime Healthcare, 29, 30, 32
private equity firms, 29–34 passim,
  76, 88, 90
psychiatric care, 56–57, 63
public employee health insurance,
  21
public health, 64–66 passim, 73;
  drug industry and, 42, 46, 51,
  104–5; international, 104–5, 111,
  119, 122
public health emergencies, 111, 119.
  See also epidemics; pandemics
puerperal fever, 18
Purdue Frederick, 37

racism, 22, 55; in medical
  experimentation, 101
research, 93–105; drugs, 43, 48–49,
  51–52, 110. *See also* clinical trials;
  medical research subjects
residents and residency, 30, 61
Rhode Island, 121; Board of
  Pharmacy, 45–46; consultants,
  70–71; COVID-19, 1–5, 70–71,
  93–94; CVS, 45; family practice,
  75, 80; nonprofit health insurers,
  85; opiates, 38, 72; orthopedic
  care, 55–56. *See also* Central Falls,
  Rhode Island

scientists' salaries, 98
Semmelweis, Ignaz, 18
smoking-cessation programs, 25, 70
specialists and specialty care, 55–66
  passim

standard of living: developing
  nations, 114
Steward Health Care, 30, 32, 33
surgery, 17, 57, 58; advertising,
  28; medical tourism, 117; as
  moneymaker, 25; surgicenters, 31
sweetheart deals, 33, 40–41, 49, 50

Tannoury, Maya, 110
teaching hospitals, 9, 61
technology, 30–31, 112–13;
  hemoglobin A1c machine, 106–8
Tenet Healthcare, 19, 30
tobacco: world market, 116–17
Tuskegee syphilis experiment, 101
Tylenol, 50

uninsured people, 61–62, 117
United Fruit (United Brands), 29–30,
  89
university-based research, 96–97;
  Kenya, 102
university hospitals, 29–30, 60,
  82–83
unnecessary health care services, 27,
  28, 32, 64, 97
urbanization: developing nations,
  109, 114

vaccines and vaccination, 39, 41, 50,
  108, 122; COVID-19, 78–79, 80,
  93–94, 111, 124–29; polio, 104
Veterans Administration, 20

"war on drugs," 36–37
workers' compensation, 33, 82
World Bank, 113, 119–20
World Trade Organization (WTO),
  110–14 passim, 119–20

Zouhair, Attieh, 110

About the Author

Michael Fine is a prize-winning fiction writer, author, community organizer, family physician, public health official, and public health policy provocateur. He is the author of *Health Care Revolt*, *Abundance*, *The Bull and Other Stories*, and *Rhode Island Stories*. He was the director of the Rhode Island Department of Health and chair of the Rhode Island Board of Medical Licensure and Discipline from 2011 to 2015 and serves as the chief health strategist for the City of Central Falls, Rhode Island.

ABOUT PM PRESS

PM Press is an independent, radical publisher of books and media to educate, entertain, and inspire. Founded in 2007 by a small group of people with decades of publishing, media, and organizing experience, PM Press amplifies the voices of radical authors, artists, and activists. Our aim is to deliver bold political ideas and vital stories to all walks of life and arm the dreamers to demand the impossible. We have sold millions of copies of our books, most often one at a time, face to face. We're old enough to know what we're doing and young enough to know what's at stake. Join us to create a better world.

PM Press
PO Box 23912
Oakland, CA 94623
www.pmpress.org

PM Press in Europe
europe@pmpress.org
www.pmpress.org.uk

FRIENDS OF PM PRESS

These are indisputably momentous times—the financial system is melting down globally and the Empire is stumbling. Now more than ever there is a vital need for radical ideas.

In the many years since its founding—and on a mere shoestring—PM Press has risen to the formidable challenge of publishing and distributing knowledge and entertainment for the struggles ahead. With hundreds of releases to date, we have published an impressive and stimulating array of literature, art, music, politics, and culture. Using every available medium, we've succeeded in connecting those hungry for ideas and information to those putting them into practice.

Friends of PM allows you to directly help impact, amplify, and revitalize the discourse and actions of radical writers, filmmakers, and artists. It provides us with a stable foundation from which we can build upon our early successes and provides a much-needed subsidy for the materials that can't necessarily pay their own way. You can help make that happen—and receive every new title automatically delivered to your door once a month—by joining as a Friend of PM Press. And, we'll throw in a free T-shirt when you sign up.

Here are your options:

- **$30 a month** Get all books and pamphlets plus 50% discount on all webstore purchases

- **$40 a month** Get all PM Press releases (including CDs and DVDs) plus 50% discount on all webstore purchases

- **$100 a month** Superstar—Everything plus PM merchandise, free downloads, and 50% discount on all webstore purchases

For those who can't afford $30 or more a month, we have **Sustainer Rates** at $15, $10 and $5. Sustainers get a free PM Press T-shirt and a 50% discount on all purchases from our website.

Your Visa or Mastercard will be billed once a month, until you tell us to stop. Or until our efforts succeed in bringing the revolution around. Or the financial meltdown of Capital makes plastic redundant. Whichever comes first.

Health Care Revolt: How to Organize, Build a Health Care System, and Resuscitate Democracy—All at the Same Time

Michael Fine
with a Foreword by Bernard Lown and
Ariel Lown Lewiton

ISBN: 978-1-62963-581-1
$15.95   192 pages

The U.S. does not have a health system. Instead we have market for health-related goods and services, a market in which the few profit from the public's ill-health.

Health Care Revolt looks around the world for examples of health care systems that are effective and affordable, pictures such a system for the U.S., and creates a practical playbook for a political revolution in health care that will allow the nation to protect health while strengthening democracy.

Dr. Fine writes with the wisdom of a clinician, the savvy of a state public health commissioner, the precision of a scholar, and the energy and commitment of a community organizer.

"This is a revolutionary book. The author incites readers to embark on an audacious revolution to convert the American medical market into the American health care system."
—T.P. Gariepy, Stonehill College/CHOICE connect

"Michael Fine is one of the true heroes of primary care over several decades."
—Dr. Doug Henley, CEO and executive vice president of the American Academy of Family Physicians

"As Rhode Island's director of health, Dr. Fine brought a vision of a humane, local, integrated health care system that focused as much on health as on disease and treatment."
—U.S. Senator Sheldon Whitehouse

"Michael Fine has given us an extraordinary biopic on health care in America based on the authority of his forty-year career as writer, community organizer, family physician, and public health official."
—Fitzhugh Mullan, MD

Abundance

Michael Fine

ISBN: 978-1-62963-644-3
$17.95   352 pages

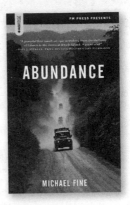

Julia is an American medical doctor fleeing her own
privileged background to find a new life delivering
health care to African villages, where her skills can
make a difference. Carl is also an American, whose
very different experiences as a black man in the
United States have driven him into exile in West
Africa, where he is an international NGO expat. The
two come together as colleagues (and then more) as Liberia is gripped in a
brutal civil war. Child soldiers kidnap Julia on a remote jungle road, and Carl
is evacuated against his will by U.S. Marines. Back in the United States he
finds Julia's mentor, Levin, a Rhode Island MD whose Sixties idealism has been
hijacked by history. Then they meet the thief. Then they meet the smuggler. And
the dangerous work of finding and rescuing Julia begins.

An unforgettable thriller grounded in real events.

"Michael Fine's novel, Abundance, is a riveting, suspenseful tale of love, violence,
adventure, idealism, sometimes-comic cynicism, class conflict and crime . . . a story
that displays both the deep disconnect between the First and Third Worlds and our
commonalities."
—Robert Whitcomb, former finance editor of the International Herald Tribune and
former editorial page editor of the Providence Journal

"Michael Fine takes us into the heart of a country at war with itself. But our journey,
in battered Land Rovers, along potholed red dirt roads, is propelled by love, not hate.
That love offers hope for Liberia, our often forgotten sister country, and anyone
who confronts despair. Read Abundance. Reignite your own search for a life worth
living."
—Martha Bebinger, WBUR

"A powerful first novel—an epic stretching from the civil wars of Liberia to the streets
of Rhode Island. A joy to read!"
—Paul J. Stekler, Emmy-winning documentary filmmaker

Crisis and Care: Queer Activist Responses to a Global Pandemic

Adrian Shanker
with a Foreword by Rea Carey

ISBN: 978-1-62963-935-2
$15.95   128 pages

Crisis and Care reveals what is possible when activists mobilize for the radical changes our society needs. In a time of great uncertainty, fear, and isolation, Queer activists organized for health equity, prison abolition, racial justice, and more. Nobody who lived through the COVID-19 pandemic will soon forget the challenges, sacrifices, and incredible loss felt during such an uncertain time in history. *Crisis and Care* anthologizes not what happened during COVID-19, or why it happened, but rather how Queer activists responded in real time. It considers the necessity to memorialize resiliency as well as loss, hope as well as pain, to remember the strides forward as well as the steps back. Activist contributors Zephyr Williams, Mark Travis Rivera, Jamie Gliksburg, Denise Spivak, Emmett Patterson, Omar Gonzales-Pagan, Kenyon Farrow, and more provide a radical lens through which future activists can consider effective strategies to make change, even or perhaps especially, during periods of crisis.

"Adrian Shanker has emerged in recent years as an urgent and prescient voice on matters concerning queer health. Crisis and Care: Queer Activist Responses to a Global Pandemic *is timely, important and shares a message we ignore at our own peril. The response to COVID-19 from LGBTQ communities is informed by our own experience with a deadly pandemic made vastly worse by poor presidential leadership. Our lived experience over the past 40 years has valuable lessons for how we should be addressing today's viral threats."*
—Sean Strub, author of *Body Counts: A Memoir of Politics, Sex, AIDS, and Survival*

"How did we respond? That is the central question in Crisis and Care. *Lots of books will look at COVID-19, but this book looks at how LGBTQ activists responded to one of the most challenging moments of our lives."*
—Igor Volsky, author of *Guns Down: How to Defeat the NRA and Build a Safer Future with Fewer Guns*

"In Crisis and Care, *Adrian Shanker and the contributing authors make the bold case that we are defined not by the bad things that happen in our society, but by how our community responds."*
—Robyn Ochs, editor of *Bi Women's Quarterly*

Bodies and Barriers: Queer Activists on Health

Adrian Shanker with a Foreword by Rachel L. Levine, MD and an Afterword by Kate Kendell

ISBN: 978-1-62963-784-6
$20.00   256 pages

LGBT people pervasively experience health disparities, affecting every part of their bodies and lives. Yet many are still grappling to understand the mutually reinforcing health care challenges that lead to worsened health outcomes. *Bodies and Barriers* informs health care professionals, students in health professions, policymakers, and fellow activists about these challenges, providing insights and a road map for action that could improve queer health.

Through artfully articulated, data-informed essays by twenty-six well-known and emerging queer activists—including Alisa Bowman, Jack Harrison-Quintana, Liz Margolies, Robyn Ochs, Sean Strub, Justin Sabia-Tanis, Ryan Thoreson, Imani Woody, and more—*Bodies and Barriers* illuminates the health challenges LGBT people experience throughout their lives and challenges conventional wisdom about health care delivery. It probes deeply into the roots of the disparities faced by those in the LGBT community and provides crucial information to fight for health equity and better health outcomes.

The contributors to *Bodies and Barriers* look for tangible improvements, drawing from the history of HIV/AIDS in the U.S. and from struggles against health care bias and discrimination. At a galvanizing moment when LGBT people have experienced great strides in lived equality, but our health as a community still lags, here is an indispensable blueprint for change by some of the most passionate and important health activists in the LGBT movement today.

"Now, more than ever, we need Bodies and Barriers *to shine a spotlight on how and why good healthcare for LGBTQ people and our families is such a challenge.* Bodies and Barriers *provides a road map for all who are ready to fight for health equity—in the doctor's office, in the halls of government, or in the streets."*
—Rea Carey, executive director, National LGBTQ Task Force

*"*Bodies and Barriers *helps LGBT community members understand the way people in the U.S. health services market erect barriers to anyone who is not the source of easy and immediate profit, and helps us all confront and break down these barriers. It helps families of LGBT people understand these obstacles and options for getting around them. And it helps health professionals hear the voices of all their patients, so that we learn to listen, and learn how to care for everyone."*
—Michael Fine, MD, former director, Rhode Island Department of Health, author of *Health Care Revolt: How to Organize, Build a Health Care System, and Resuscitate Democracy All at the Same Time*

Birth Work as Care Work: Stories from Activist Birth Communities

Alana Apfel, with a Foreword by Loretta J. Ross, Preface by Victoria Law, and Introduction by Silvia Federici

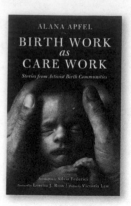

ISBN: 978-1-62963-151-6
$14.95   128 pages

Birth Work as Care Work presents a vibrant collection of stories and insights from the front lines of birth activist communities. The personal has once more become political, and birth workers, supporters, and doulas now find themselves at the fore of collective struggles for freedom and dignity.

The author, herself a scholar and birth justice organiser, provides a unique platform to explore the political dynamics of birth work; drawing connections between birth, reproductive labor, and the struggles of caregiving communities today. Articulating a politics of care work in and through the reproductive process, the book brings diverse voices into conversation to explore multiple possibilities and avenues for change.

At a moment when agency over our childbirth experiences is increasingly centralized in the hands of professional elites, *Birth Work as Care Work* presents creative new ways to reimagine the trajectory of our reproductive processes. Most importantly, the contributors present new ways of thinking about the entire life cycle, providing a unique and creative entry point into the essence of all human struggle—the struggle over the reproduction of life itself.

"I love this book, all of it. The polished essays and the interviews with birth workers dare to take on the deepest questions of human existence."
—Carol Downer, cofounder of the Feminist Women's Heath Centers of California and author of *A Woman's Book of Choices*

"This volume provides theoretically rich, practical tools for birth and other care workers to collectively and effectively fight capitalism and the many intersecting processes of oppression that accompany it. Birth Work as Care Work *forcefully and joyfully reminds us that the personal is political, a lesson we need now more than ever."*
—Adrienne Pine, author of *Working Hard, Drinking Hard: On Violence and Survival in Honduras*

Don't Leave Your Friends Behind: Concrete Ways to Support Families in Social Justice Movements and Communities

Edited by Victoria Law and
China Martens

ISBN: 978-1-60486-396-3
$17.95   256 pages

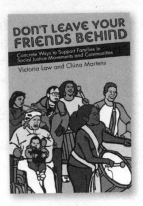

Don't Leave Your Friends Behind is a collection of concrete tips, suggestions, and narratives on ways that non-parents can support parents, children, and caregivers in their communities, social movements, and collective processes. *Don't Leave Your Friends Behind* focuses on issues affecting children and caregivers within the larger framework of social justice, mutual aid, and collective liberation.

How do we create new, nonhierarchical structures of support and mutual aid, and include all ages in the struggle for social justice? There are many books on parenting, but few on being a good community member and a good ally to parents, caregivers, and children as we collectively build a strong all-ages culture of resistance. Any group of parents will tell you how hard their struggles are and how they are left out, but no book focuses on how allies can address issues of caretakers' and children's oppression. Many well-intentioned childless activists don't interact with young people on a regular basis and don't know how. *Don't Leave Your Friends Behind* provides them with the resources and support to get started.

Contributors include: The Bay Area Childcare Collective, Ramsey Beyer, Rozalinda Borcilă, Mariah Boone, Marianne Bullock, Lindsey Campbell, Briana Cavanaugh, CRAP! Collective, a de la maza pérez tamayo, Ingrid DeLeon, Clayton Dewey, David Gilbert, A.S. Givens, Jason Gonzales, Tiny (aka Lisa Gray-Garcia), Jessica Hoffman, Heather Jackson, Rahula Janowski, Sine Hwang Jensen, Agnes Johnson, Simon Knaphus, Victoria Law, London Pro-Feminist Men's Group, Amariah Love, Oluko Lumumba, mama raccoon, Mamas of Color Rising/Young Women United, China Martens, Noemi Martinez, Kathleen McIntyre, Stacey Milbern, Jessica Mills, Tomas Moniz, Coleen Murphy, Maegan 'la Mamita Mala' Ortiz, Traci Picard, Amanda Rich, Fabiola Sandoval, Cynthia Ann Schemmer, Mikaela Shafer, Mustafa Shakur, Kate Shapiro, Jennifer Silverman, Harriet Moon Smith, Mariahadessa Ekere Tallie, Darran White Tilghman, Jessica Trimbath, Max Ventura, and Mari Villaluna.

My Baby Rides the Short Bus: The Unabashedly Human Experience of Raising Kids with Disabilities

Edited by Yantra Bertelli, Jennifer Silverman, and Sarah Talbot

ISBN: 978-1-60486-109-9
$20.00   336 pages

In lives where there is a new diagnosis or drama every day, the stories in this collection provide parents of "special needs" kids with a welcome chuckle, a rock to stand on, and a moment of reality held far enough from the heart to see clearly. Featuring works by "alternative" parents who have attempted to move away from mainstream thought—or remove its influence altogether—this anthology, taken as a whole, carefully considers the implications of parenting while raising children with disabilities.

From professional writers to novice storytellers including Robert Rummel-Hudson, Ayun Halliday, and Kerry Cohen, this assortment of authentic, shared experiences from parents at the fringe of the fringes is a partial antidote to the stories that misrepresent, ridicule, and objectify disabled kids and their parents.

"This is a collection of beautifully written stories, incredibly open and well articulated, complicated and diverse: about human rights and human emotions. About love, and difficulties; informative and supportive. Wise, non-conformist, and absolutely punk rock!"
— China Martens, author of *The Future Generation: The Zine-Book for Subculture Parents, Kids, Friends and Others*

"If only that lady in the grocery store and all of those other so-called parenting experts would read this book! These true-life tales by mothers and fathers raising kids with 'special needs' on the outer fringes of mainstream America are by turns empowering, heartbreaking, inspiring, maddening, and even humorous. Readers will be moved by the bold honesty of these voices, and by the fierce love and determination that rings throughout. This book is a vital addition to the public discourse on disability."
— Suzanne Kamata, editor of *Love You to Pieces: Creative Writers on Raising a Child with Special Needs*

"This is the most important book I've read in years. Whether you are subject or ally, My Baby Rides the Short Bus will open you—with its truth, humanity, and poetry. Lucky you to have found it. Now stick it in your heart."
— Ariel Gore, founding editor of *Hip Mama*